Charlotte Lybeer
Epidermis II

04

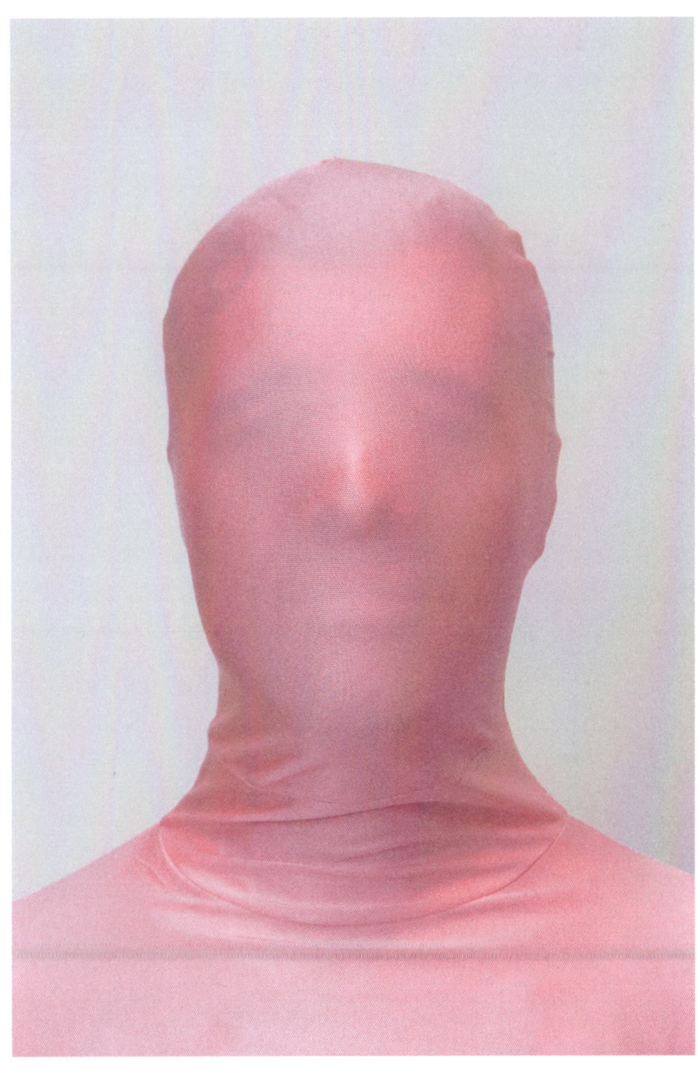

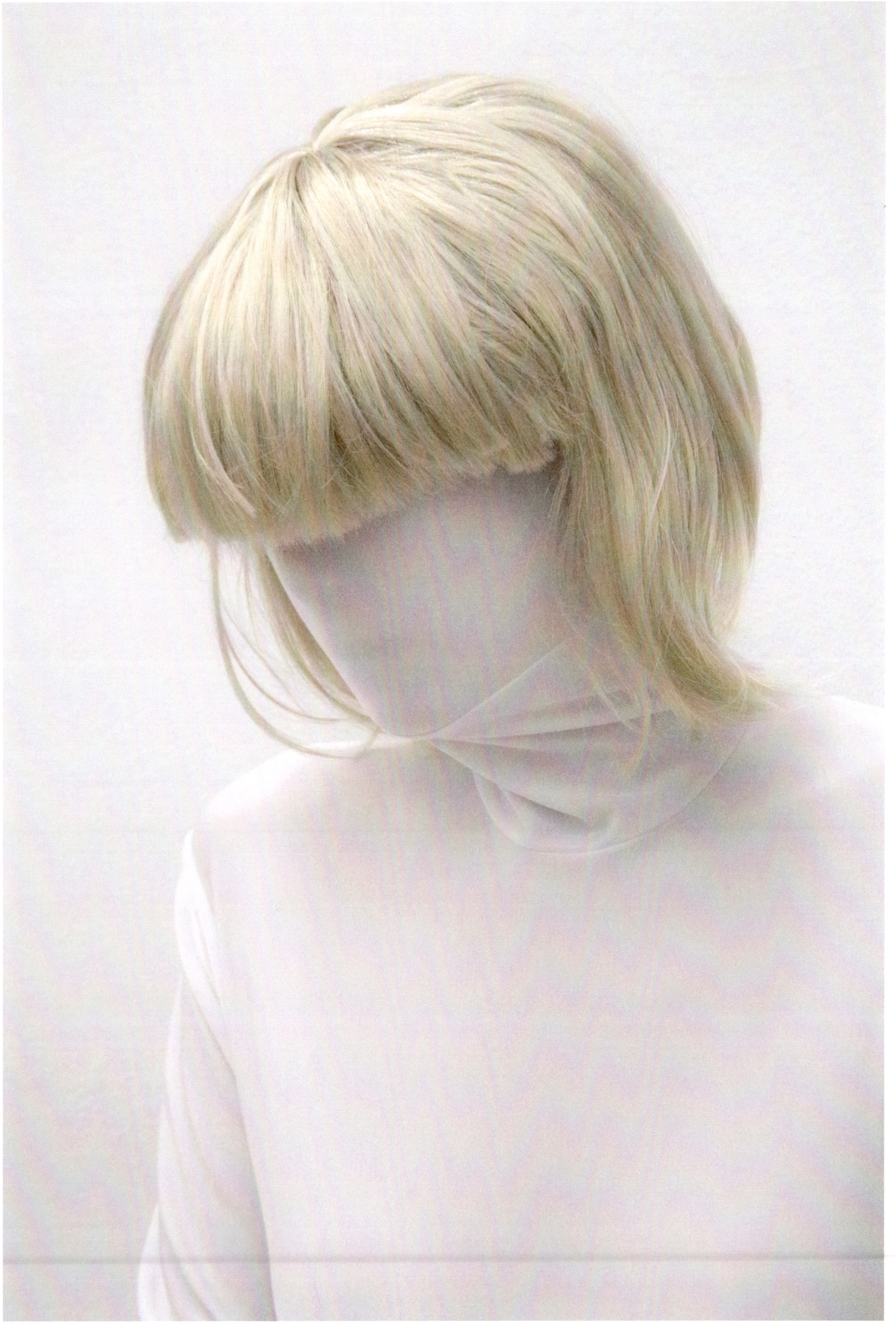

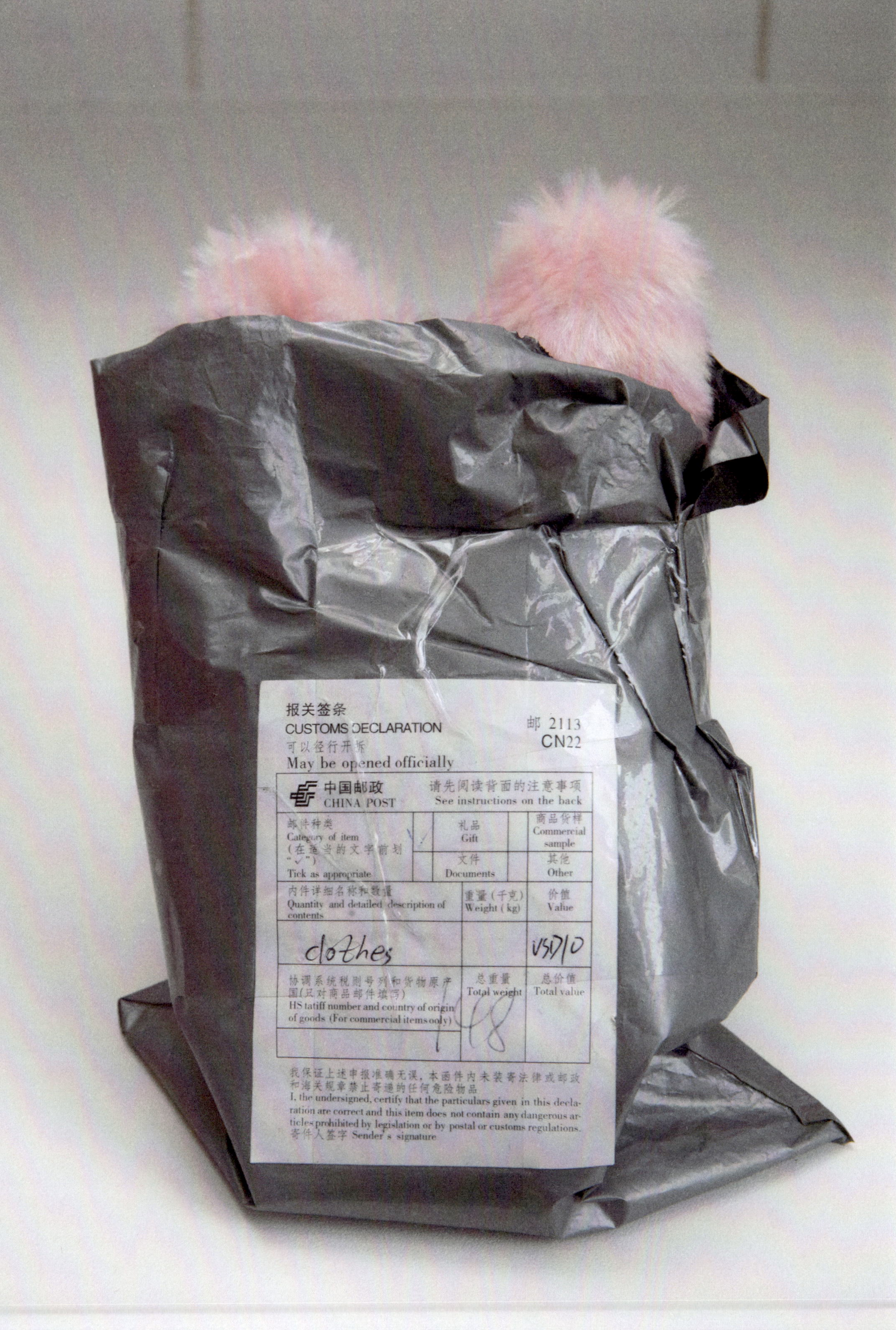
报关签条
CUSTOMS DECLARATION
邮 2113
CN22
可以径行开拆
May be opened officially
中国邮政
CHINA POST
请先阅读背面的注意事项
See instructions on the back
邮件种类
Category of item
(在适当的文字前划"✓")
Tick as appropriate
礼品
Gift
商品货样
Commercial sample
文件
Documents
其他
Other
内件详细名称和数量
Quantity and detailed description of contents
重量(千克)
Weight (kg)
价值
Value
clothes
USD10
协调系统税则号列和货物原产国(只对商品邮件填写)
HS tatiff number and country of origin of goods (For commercial items ooly)
总重量
Total weight
总价值
Total value
我保证上述申报准确无误，本函件内未装寄法律或邮政和海关规章禁止寄递的任何危险物品
I, the undersigned, certify that the particulars given in this declaration are correct and this item does not contain any dangerous articles prohibited by legislation or by postal or customs regulations.
寄件人签字 Sender's signature

07

08

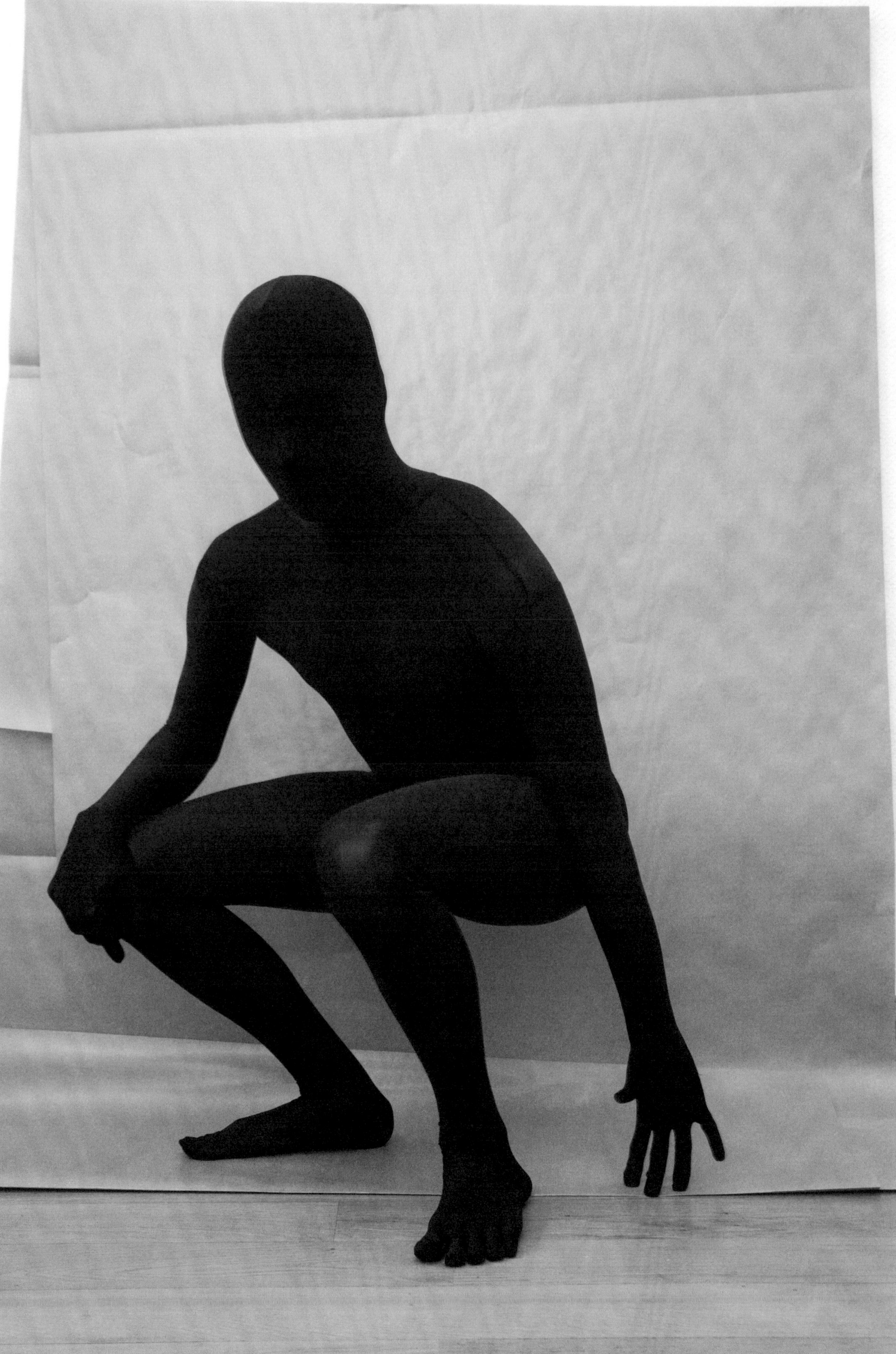

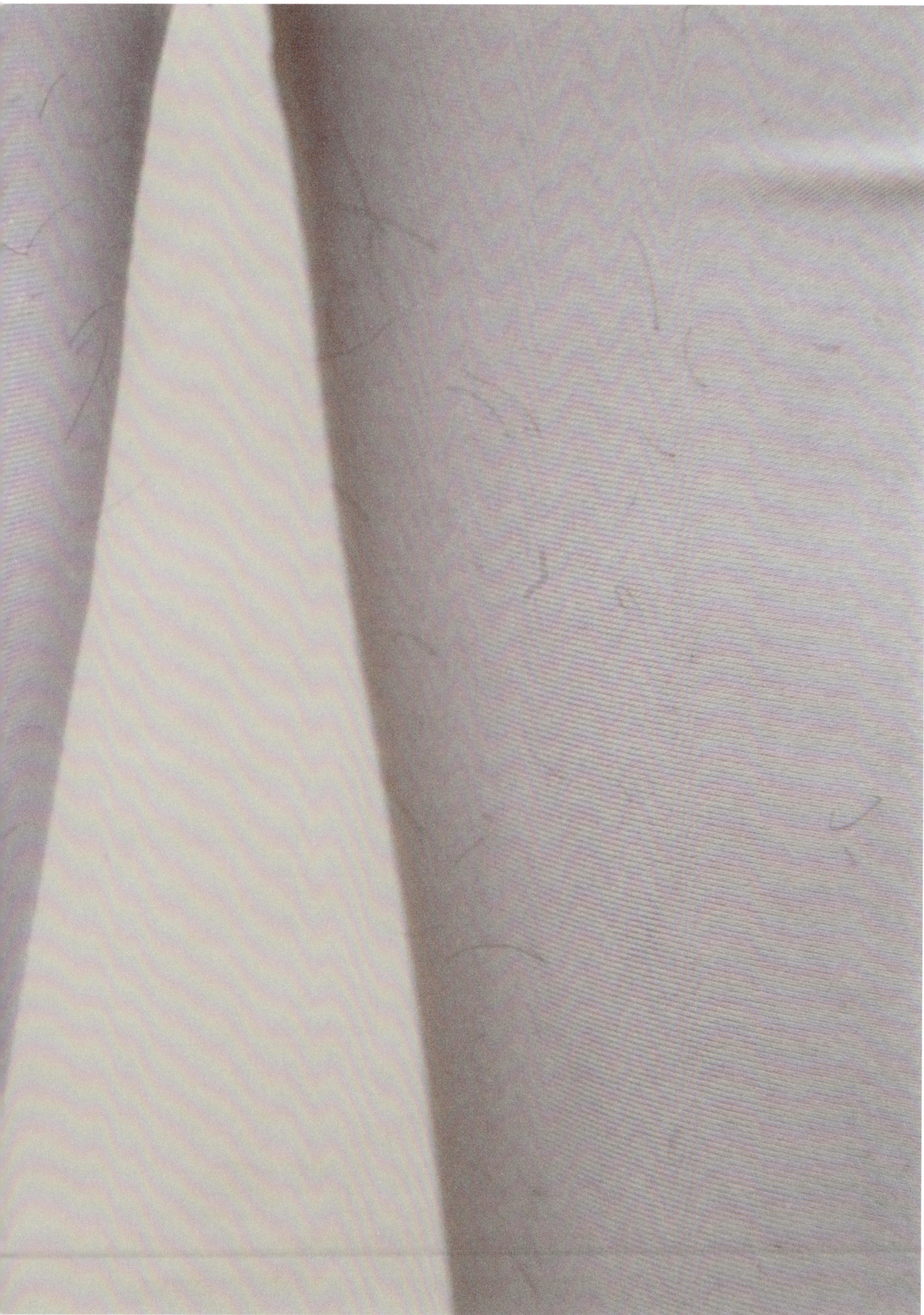

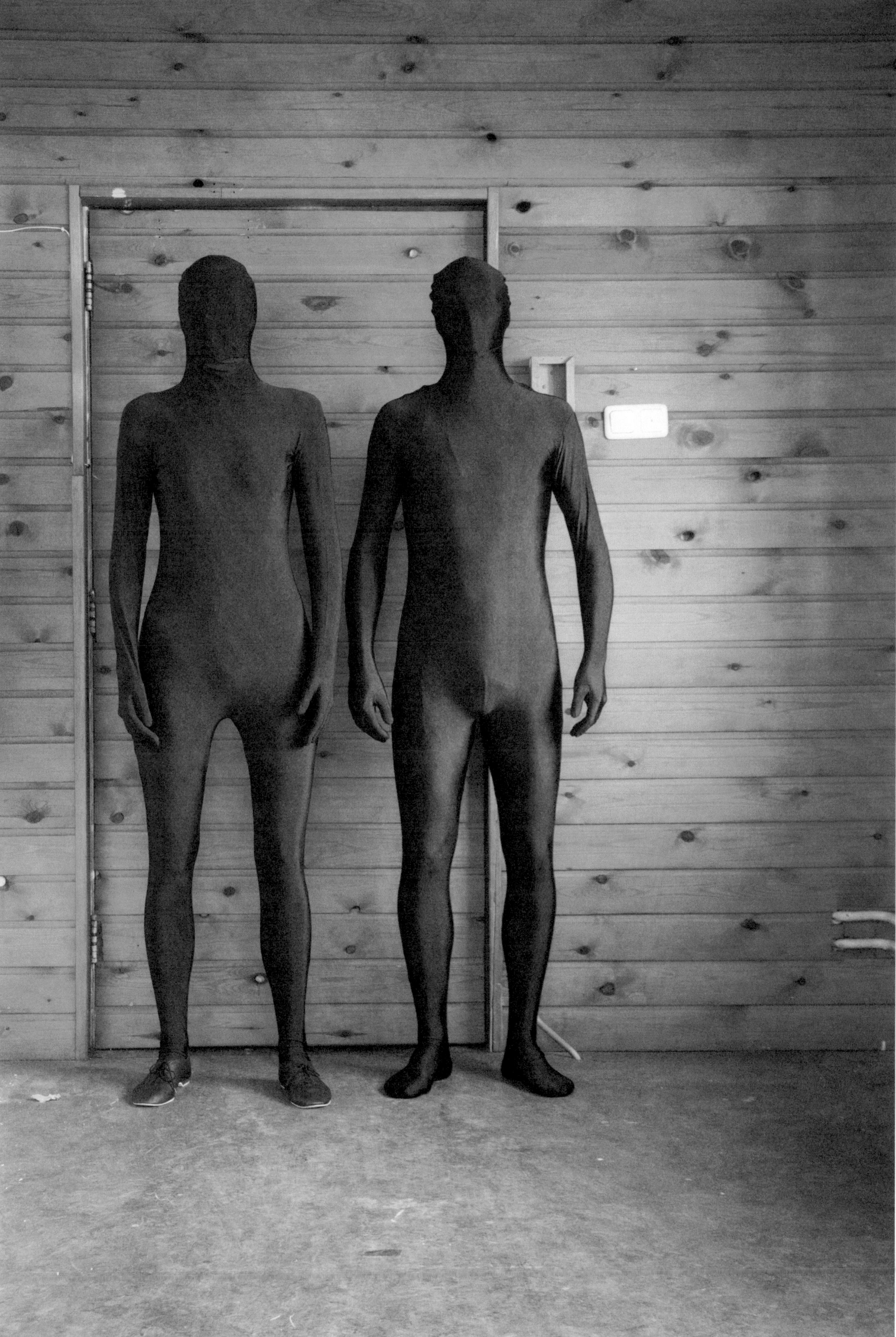

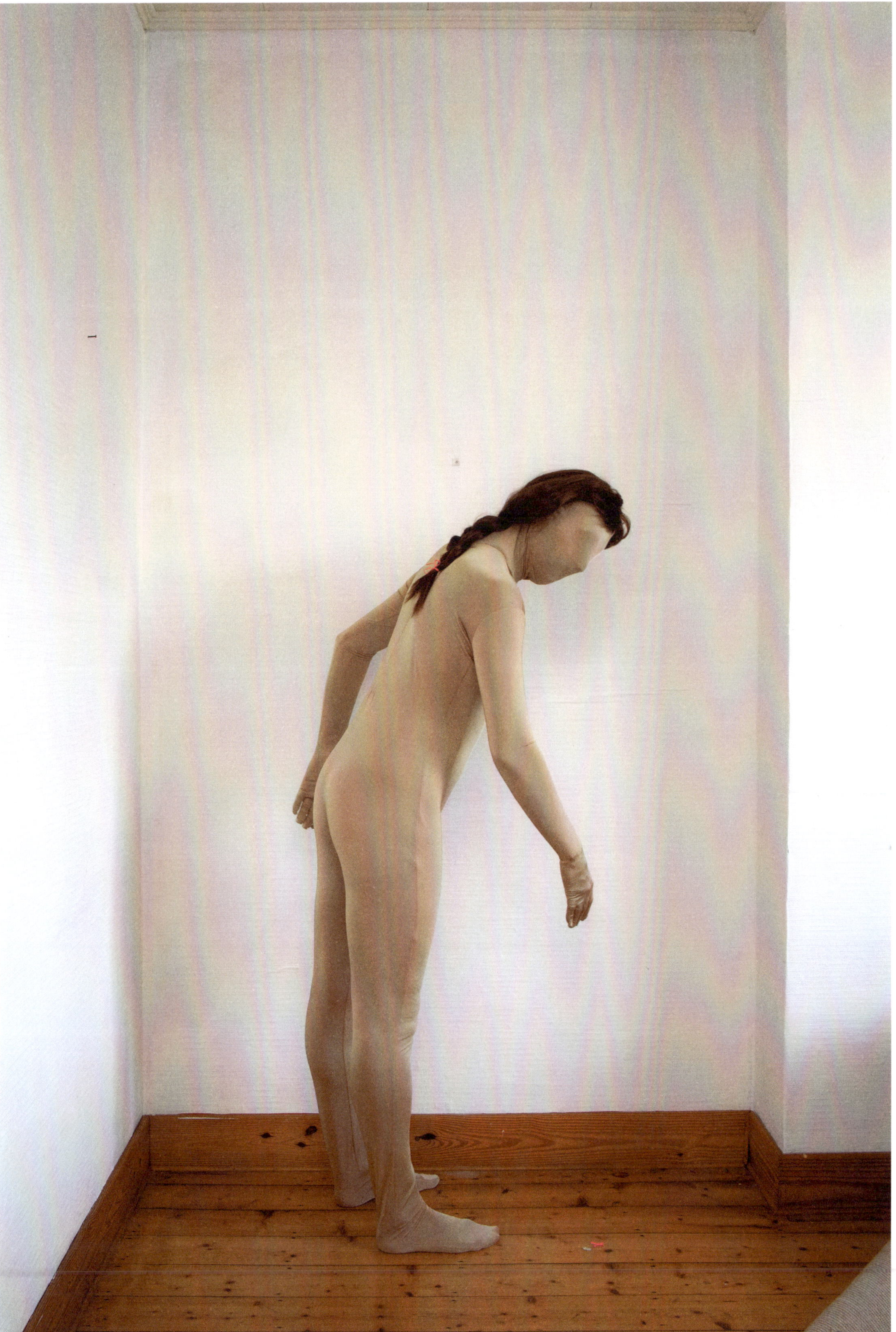

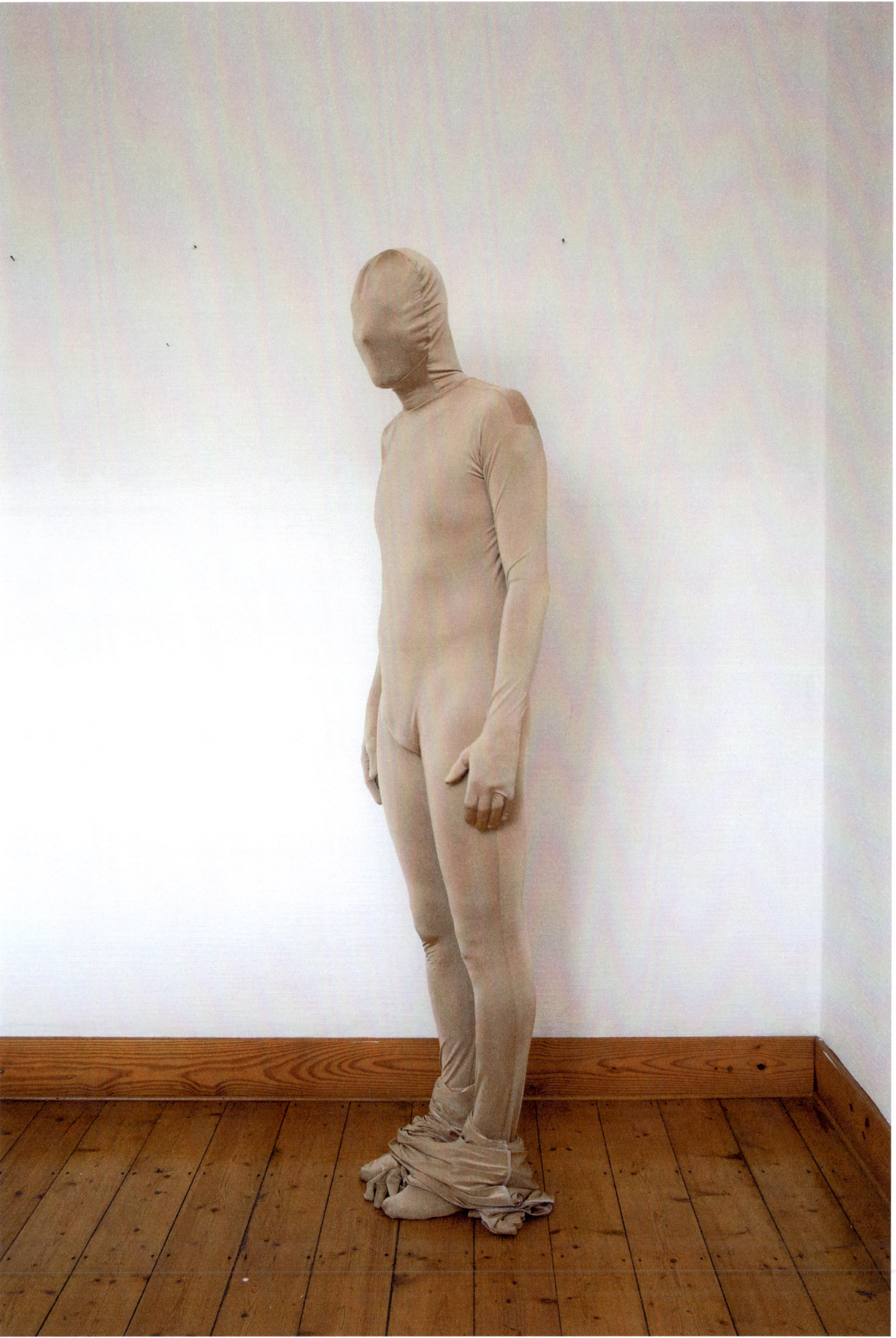

12

13 14

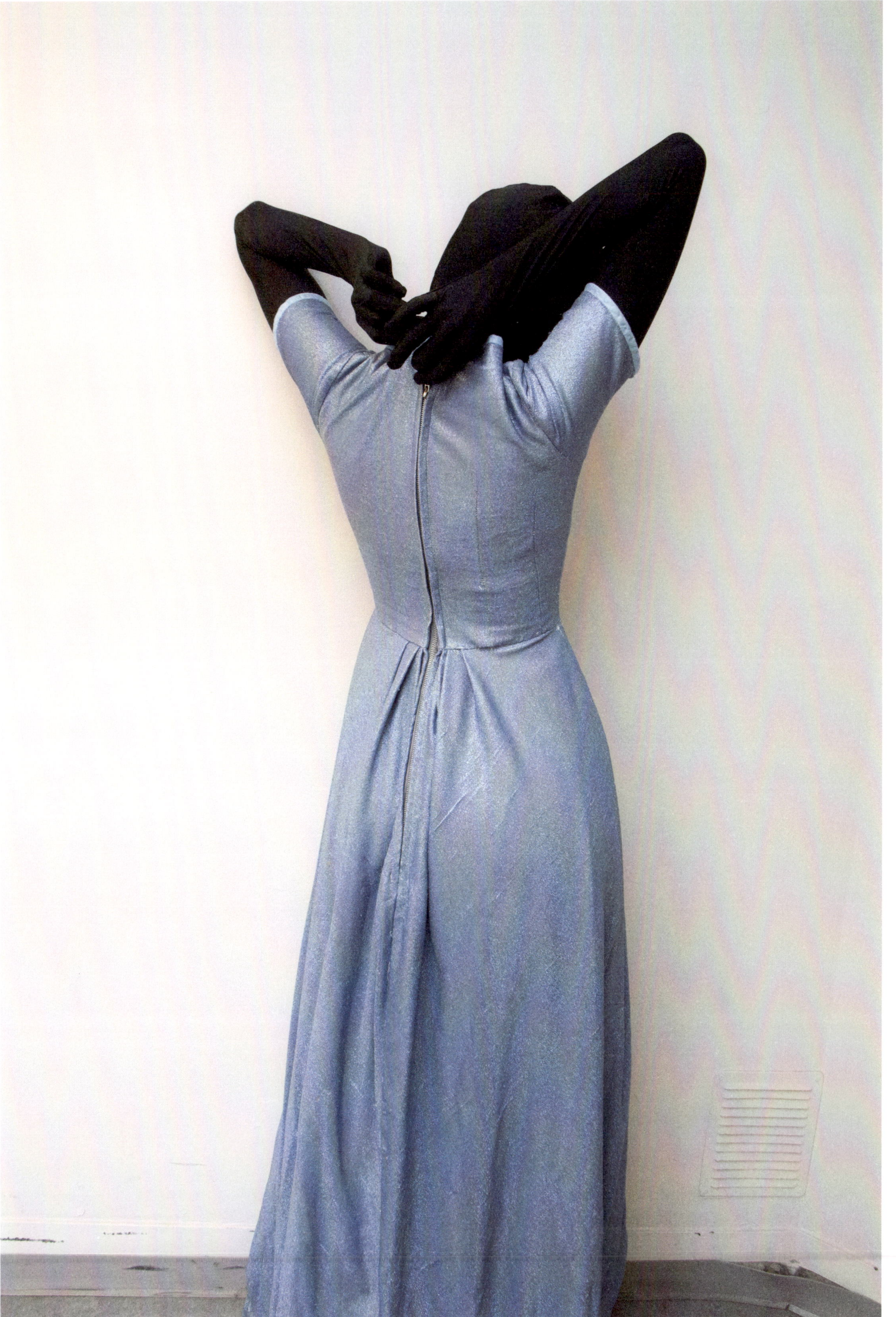

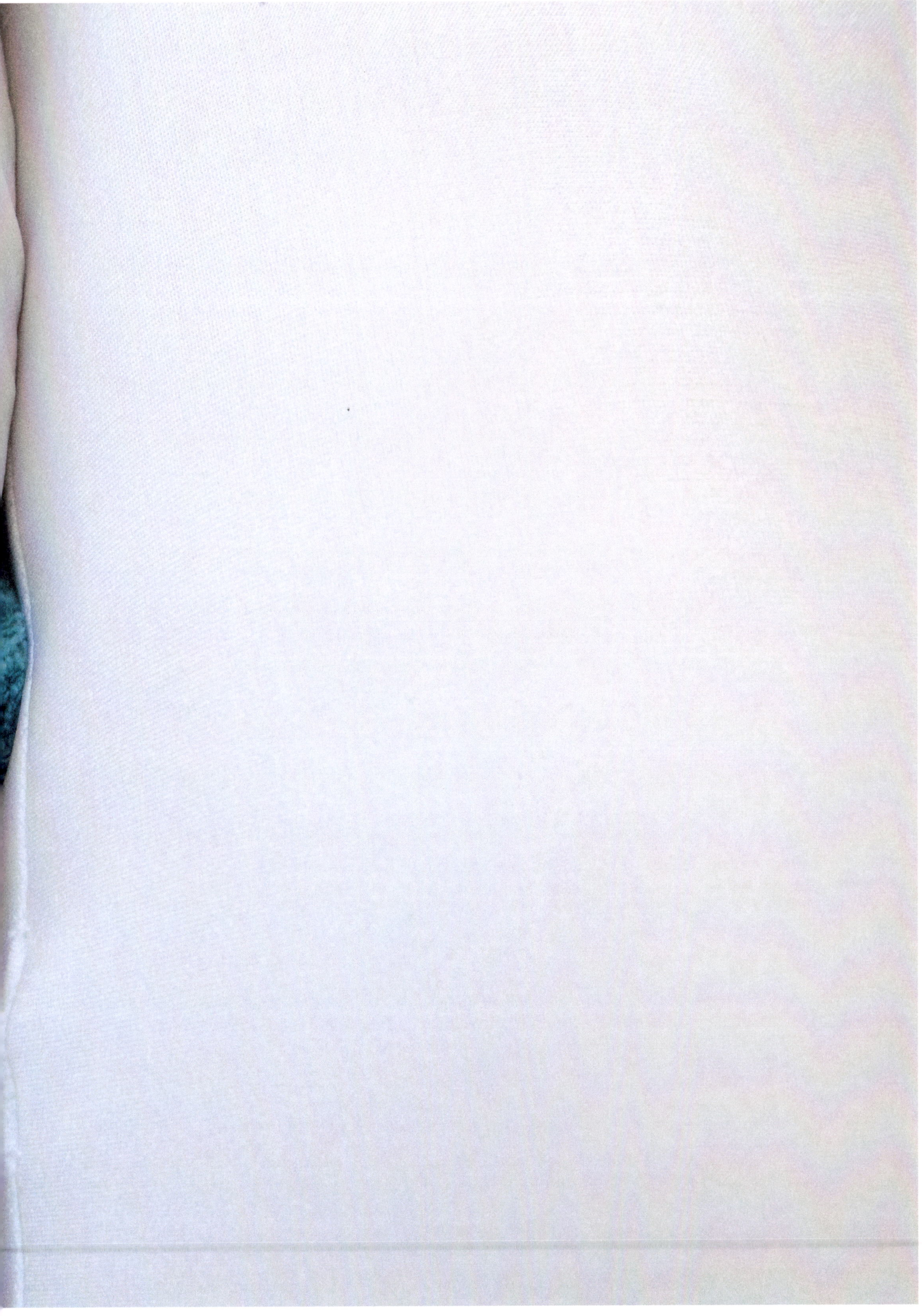

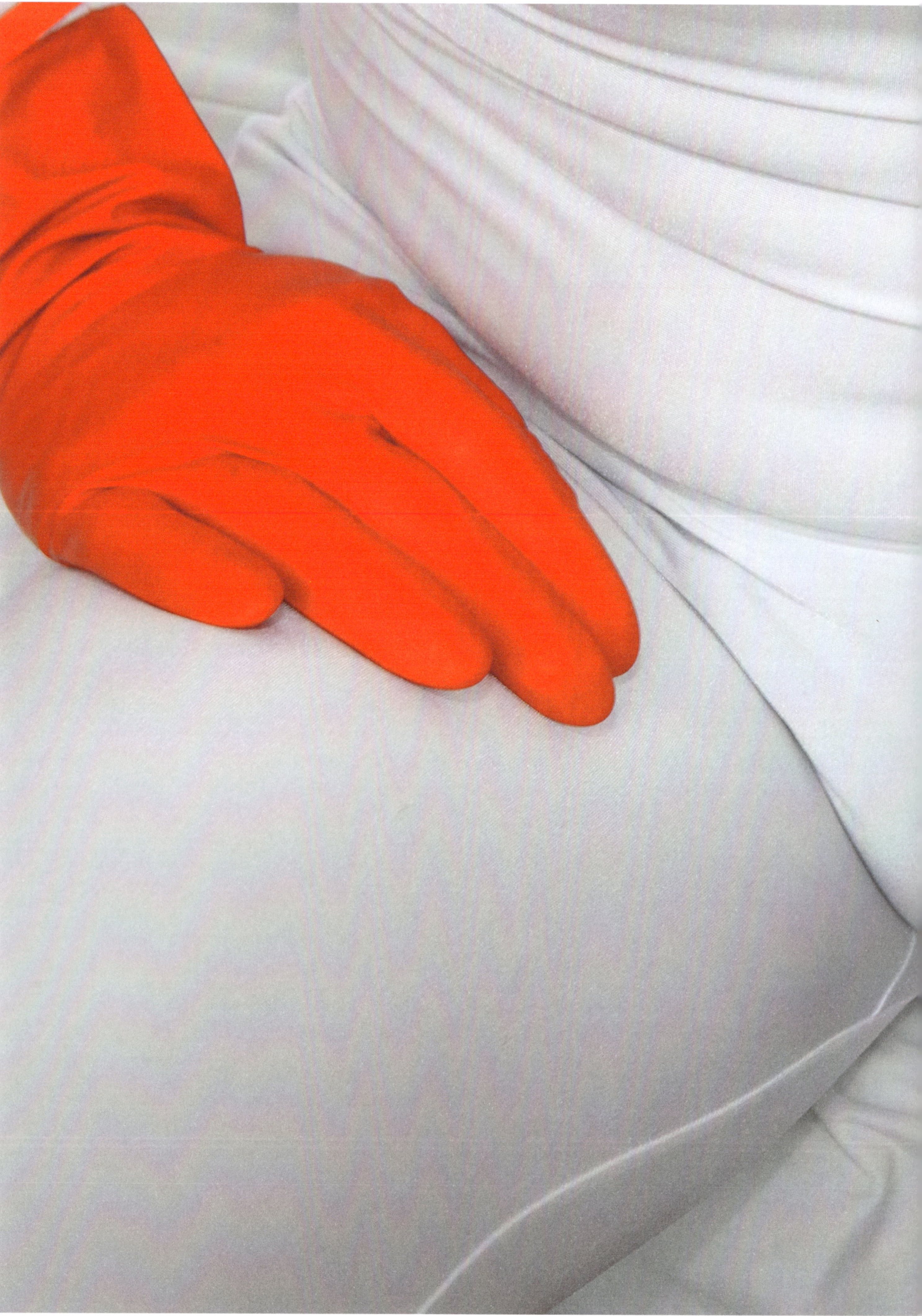

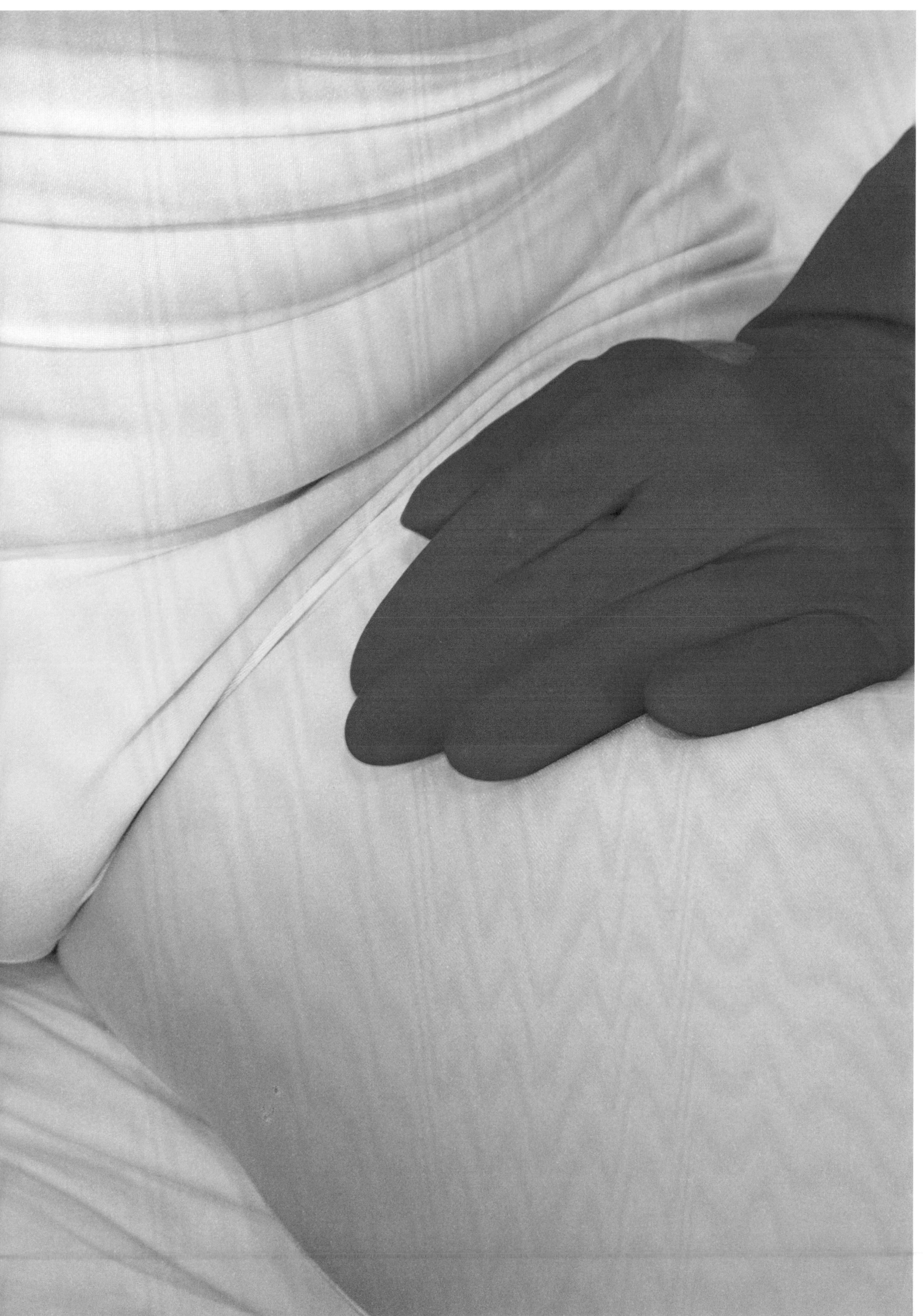

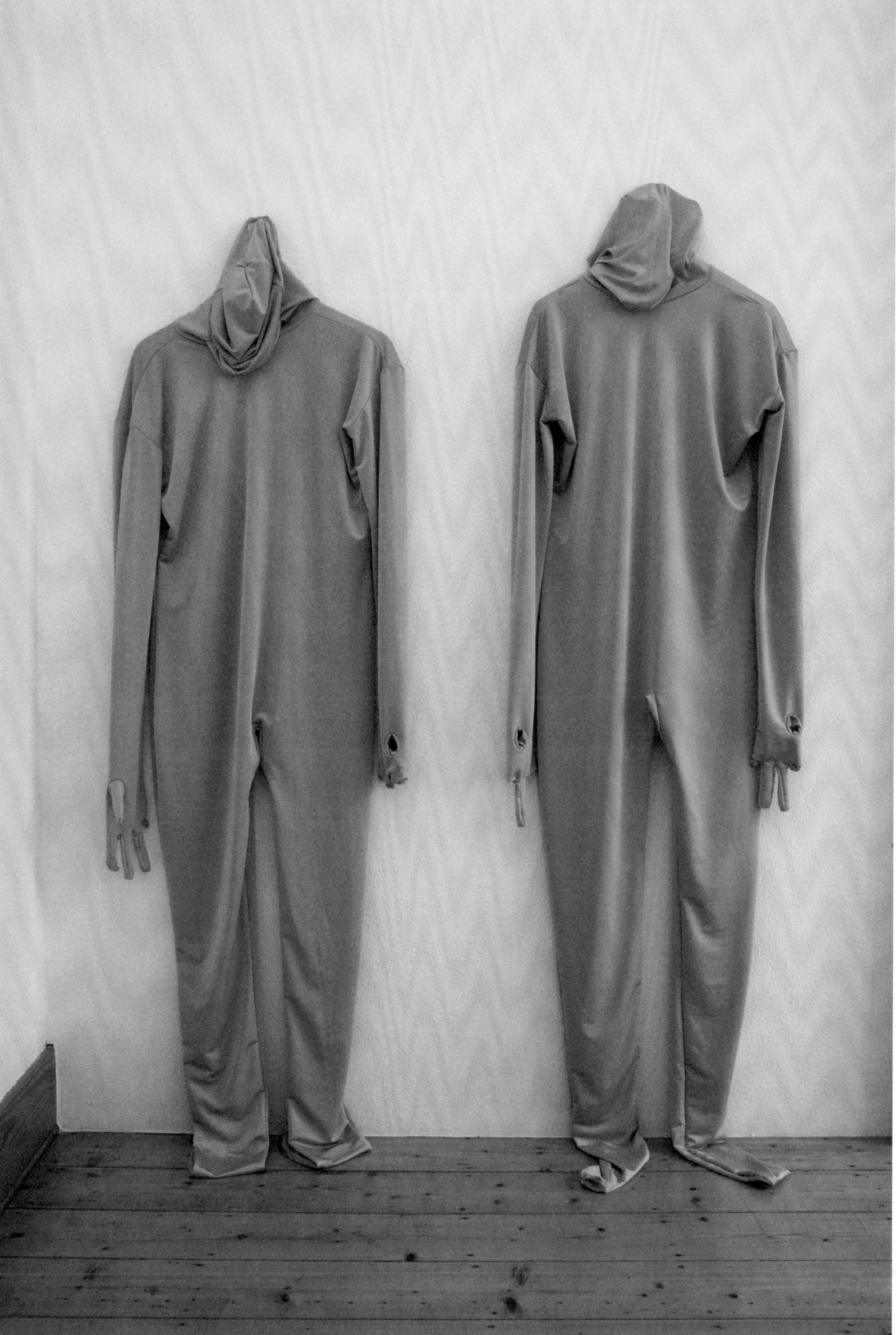

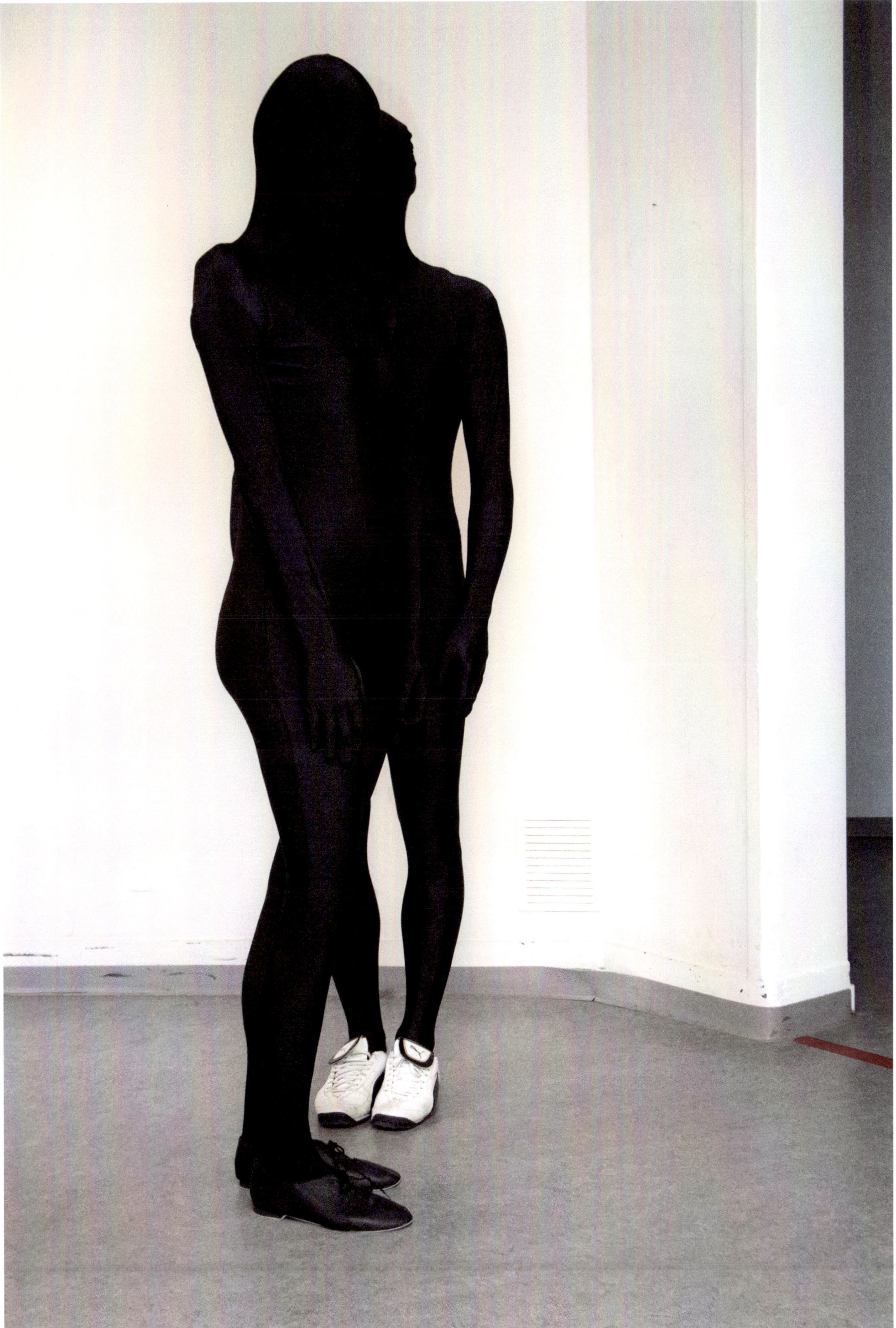

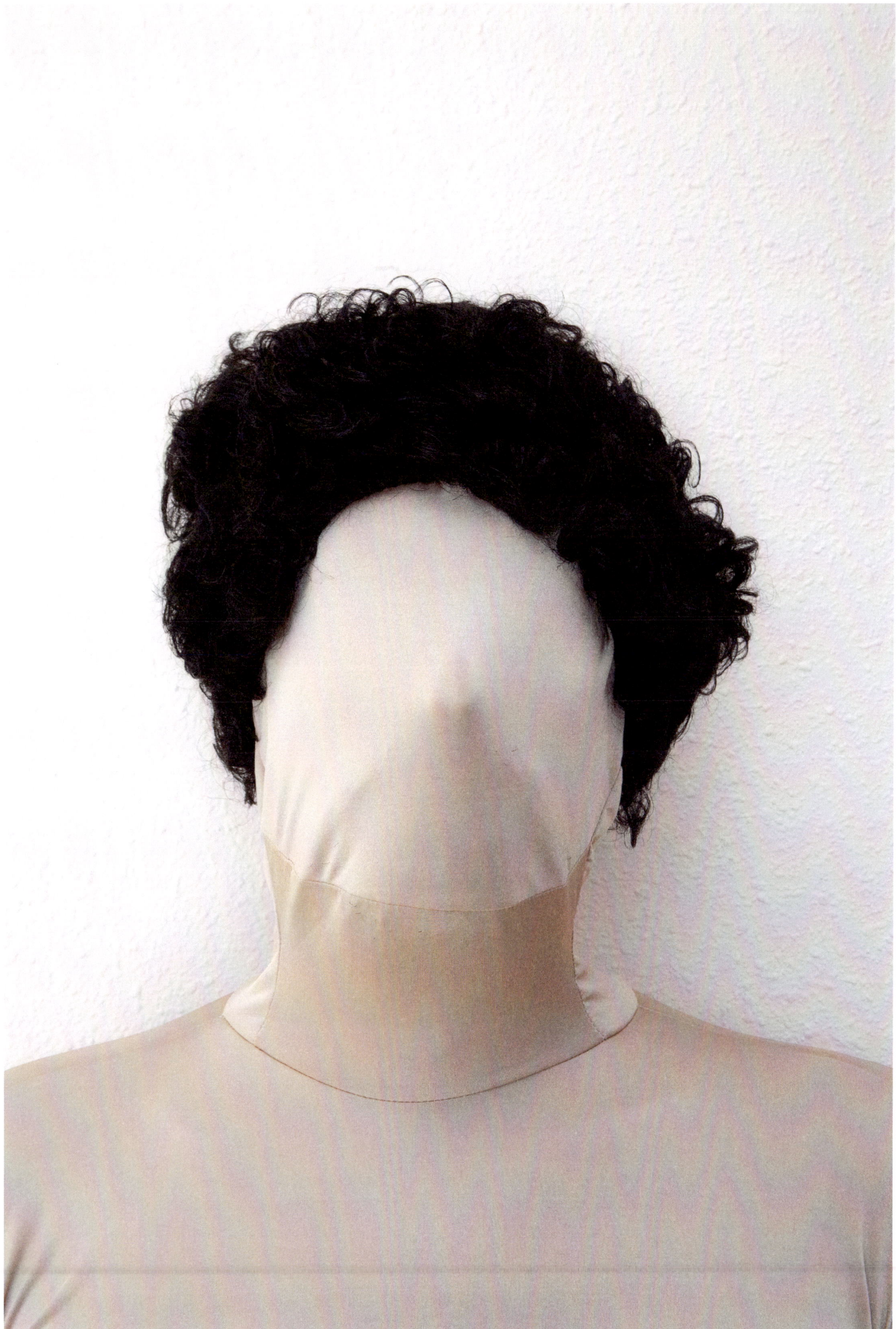

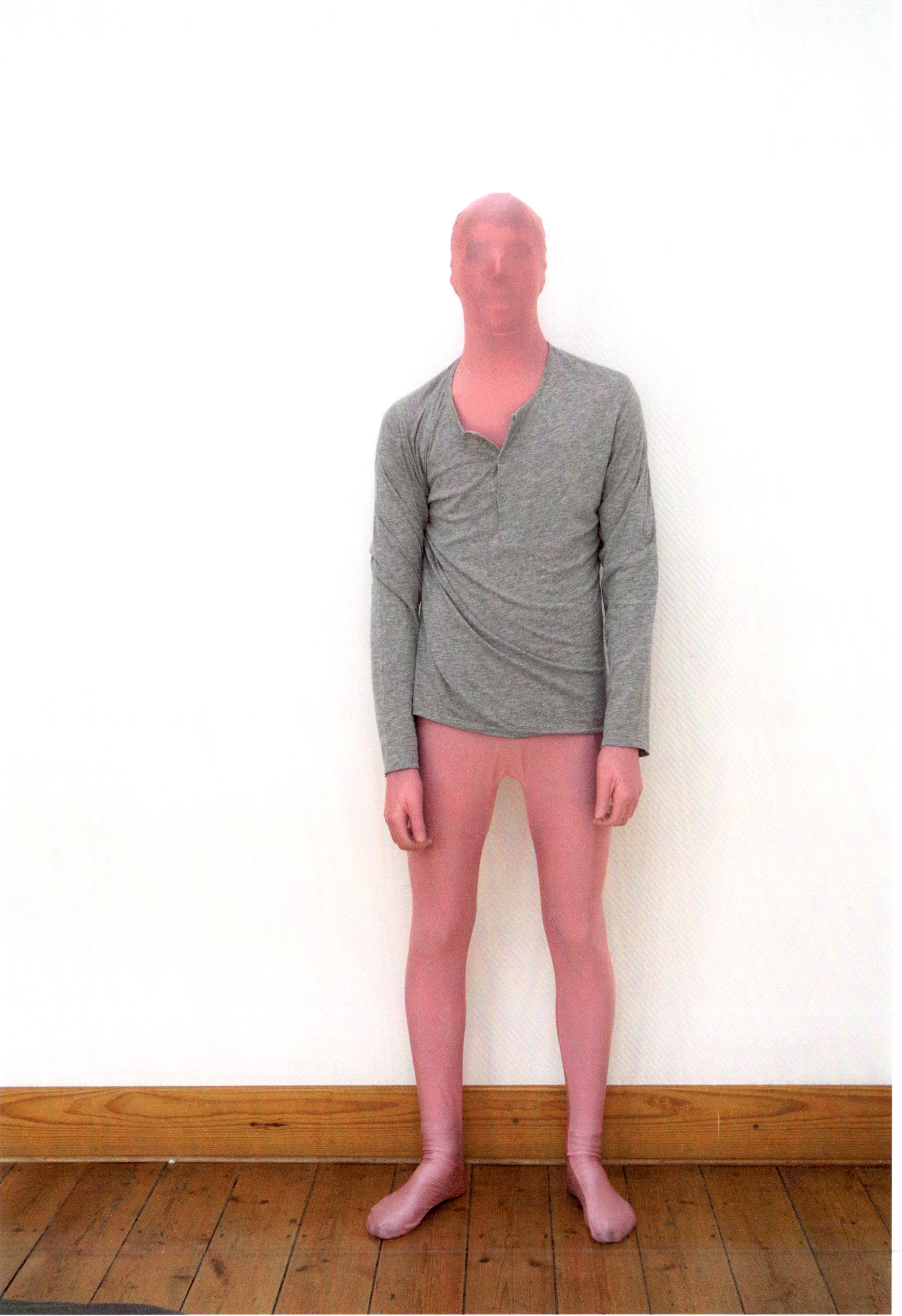

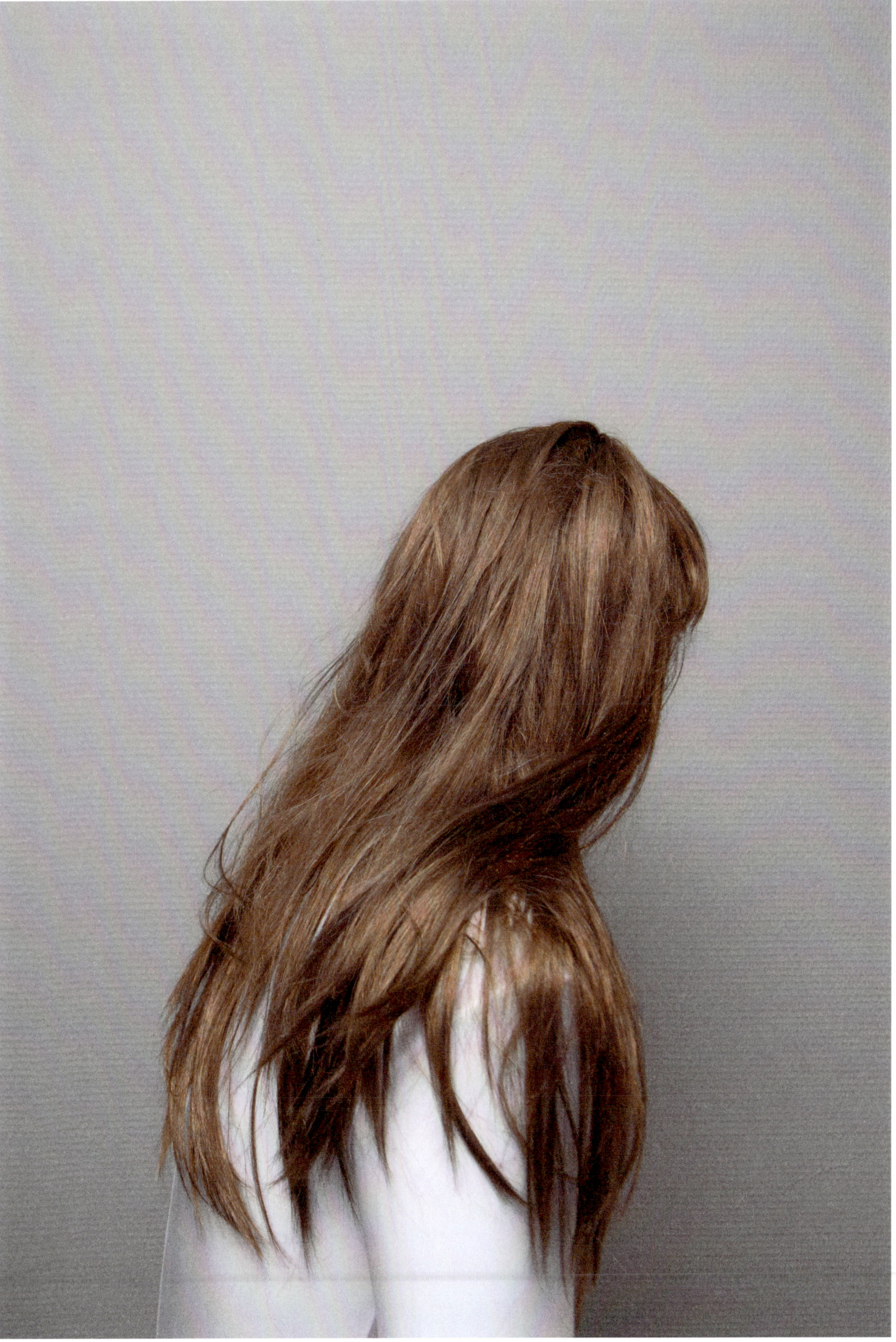

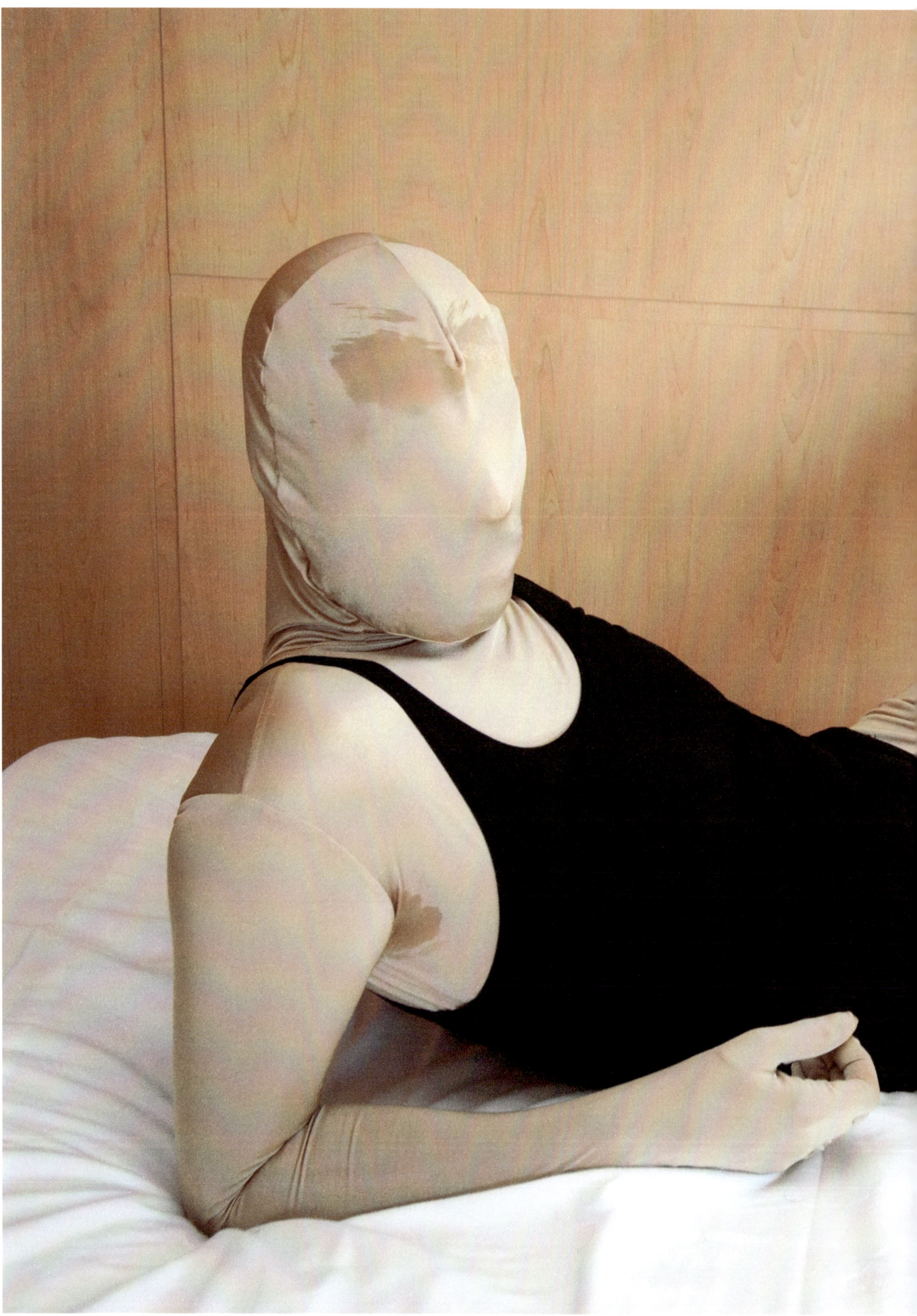

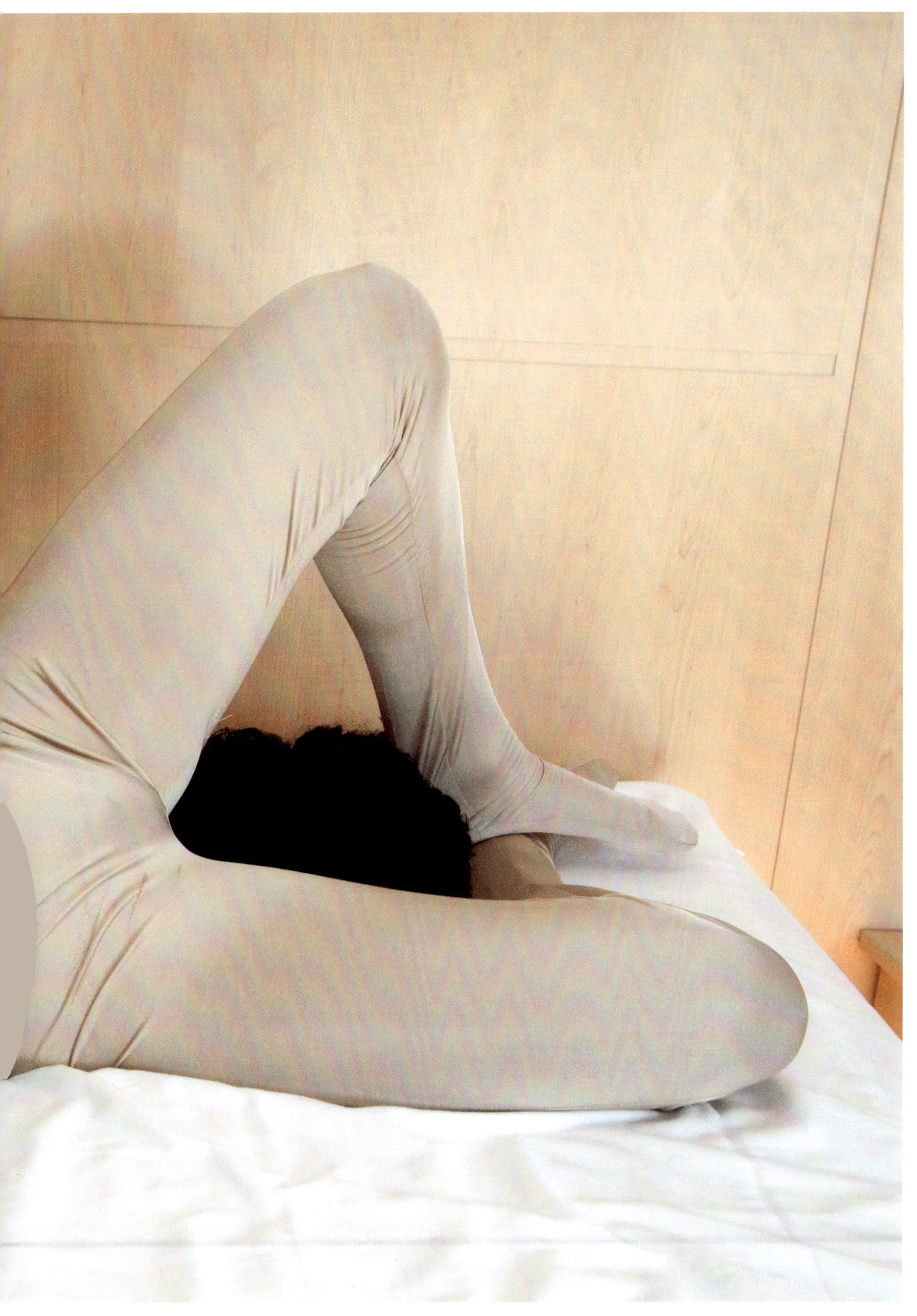

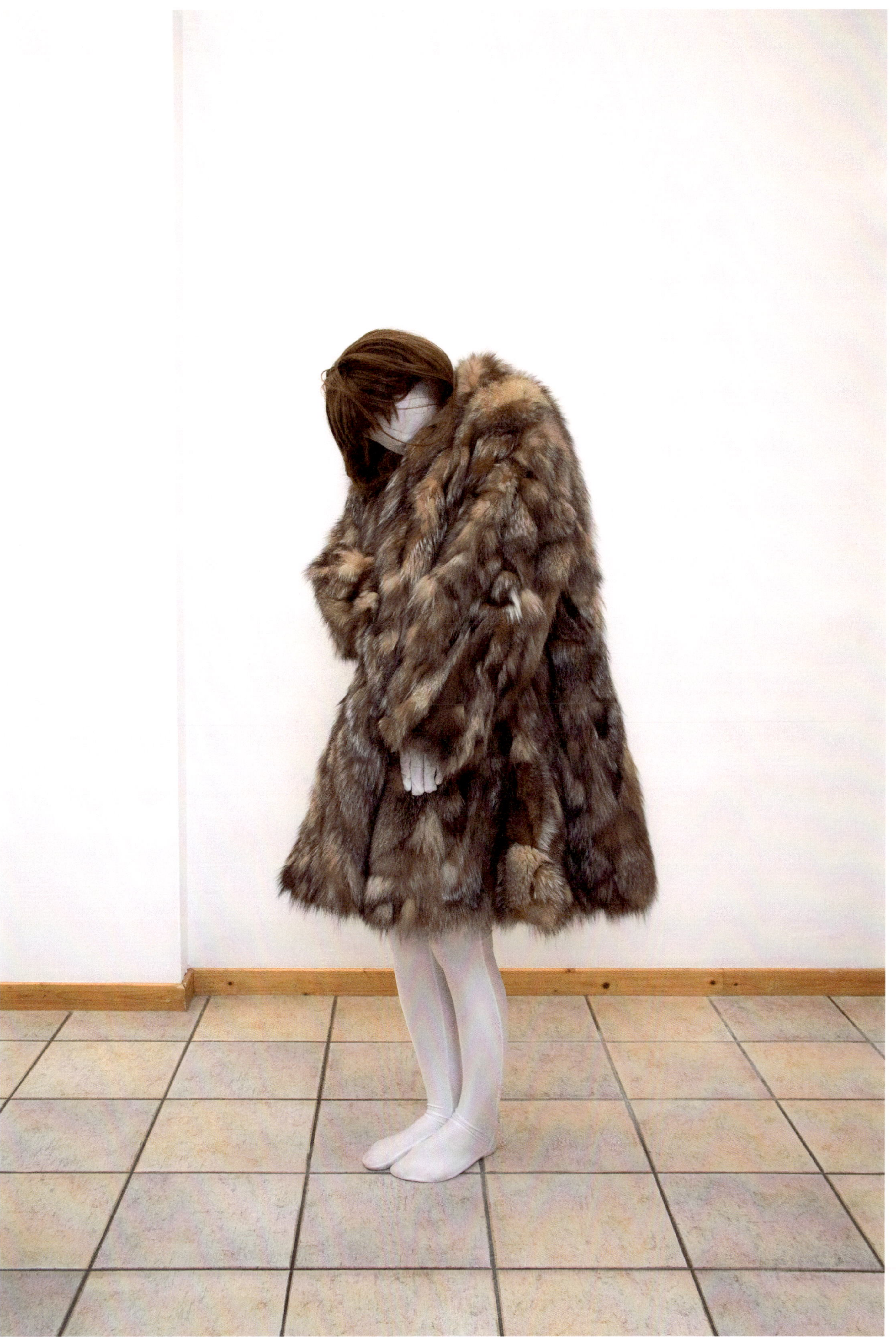

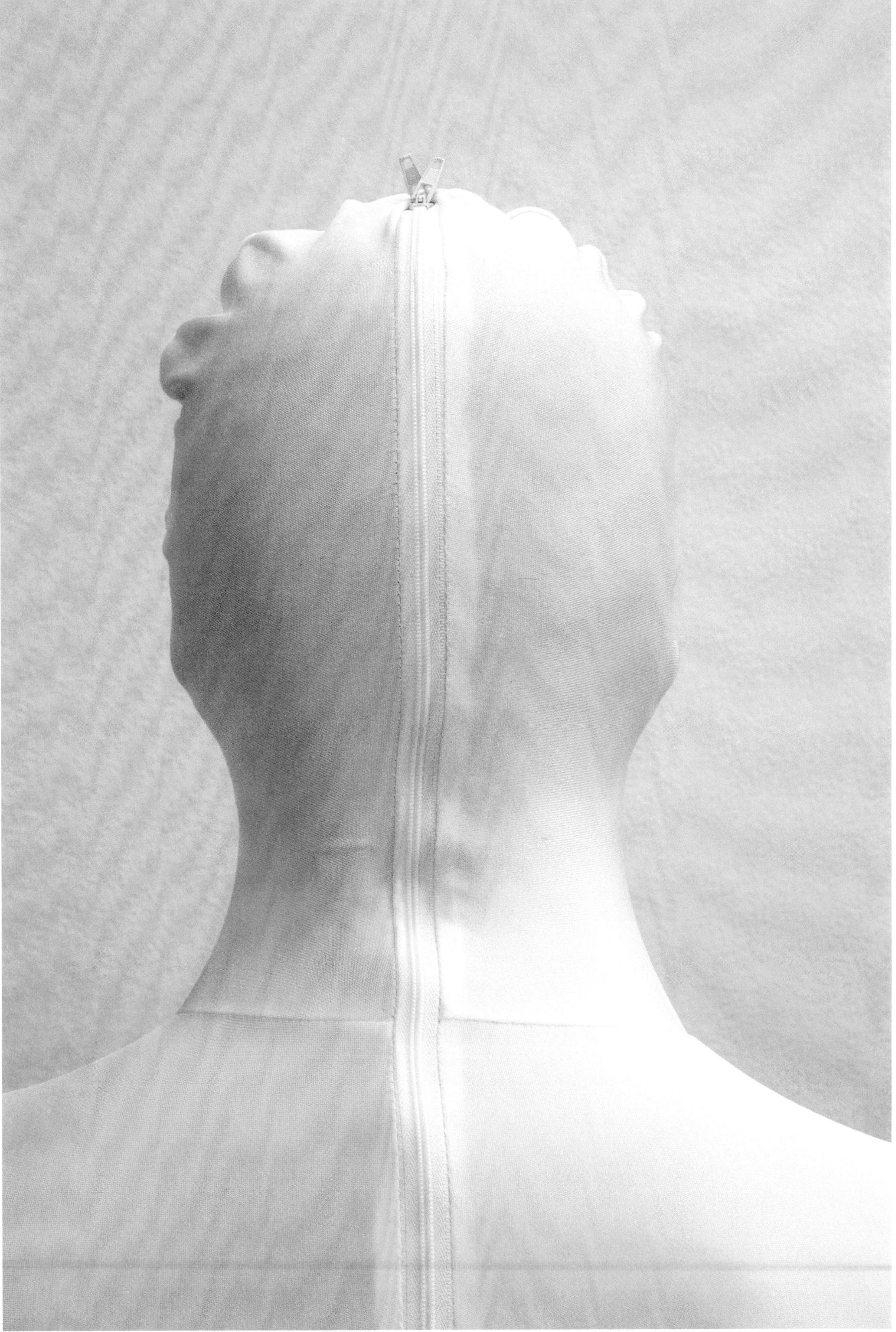

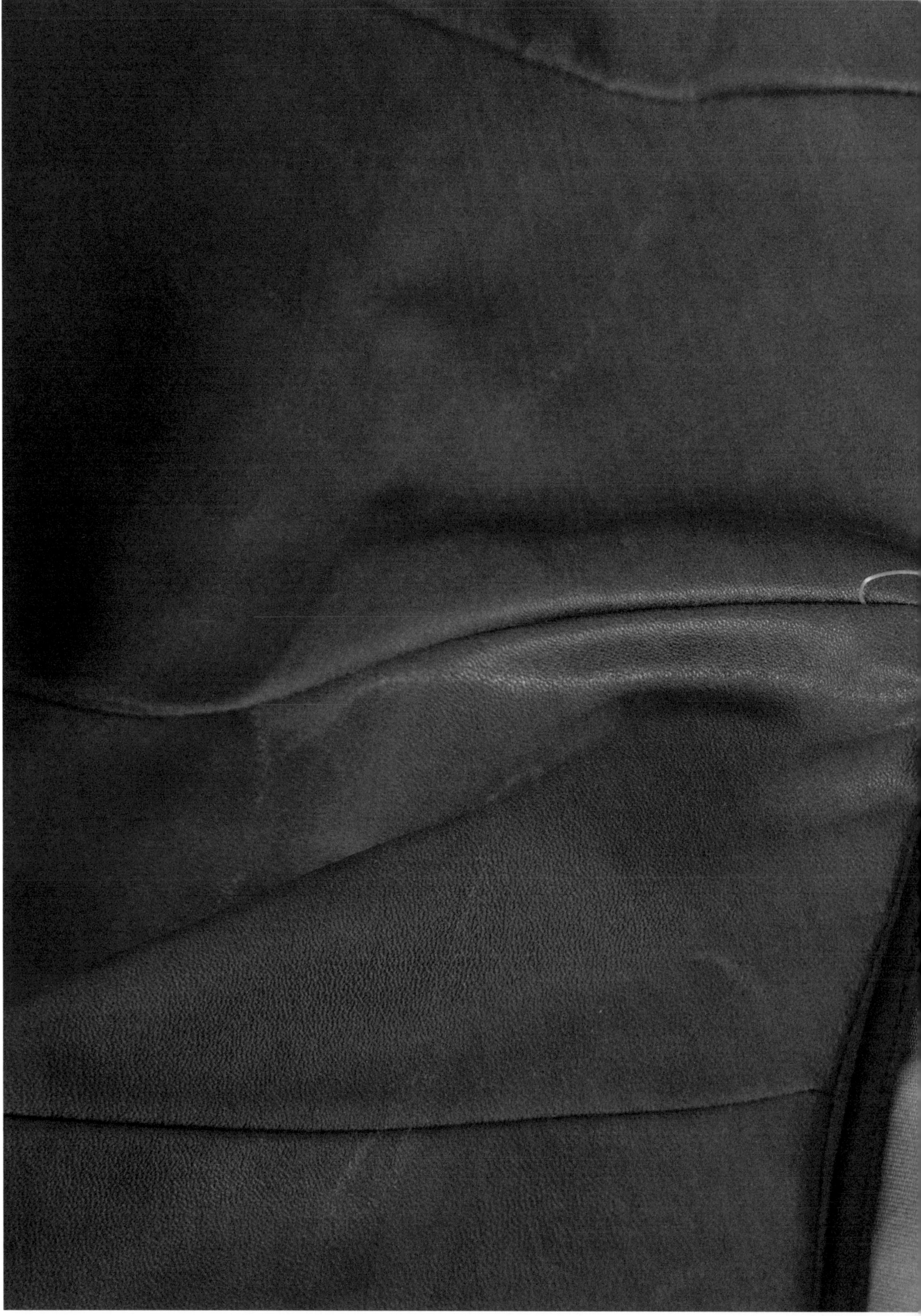

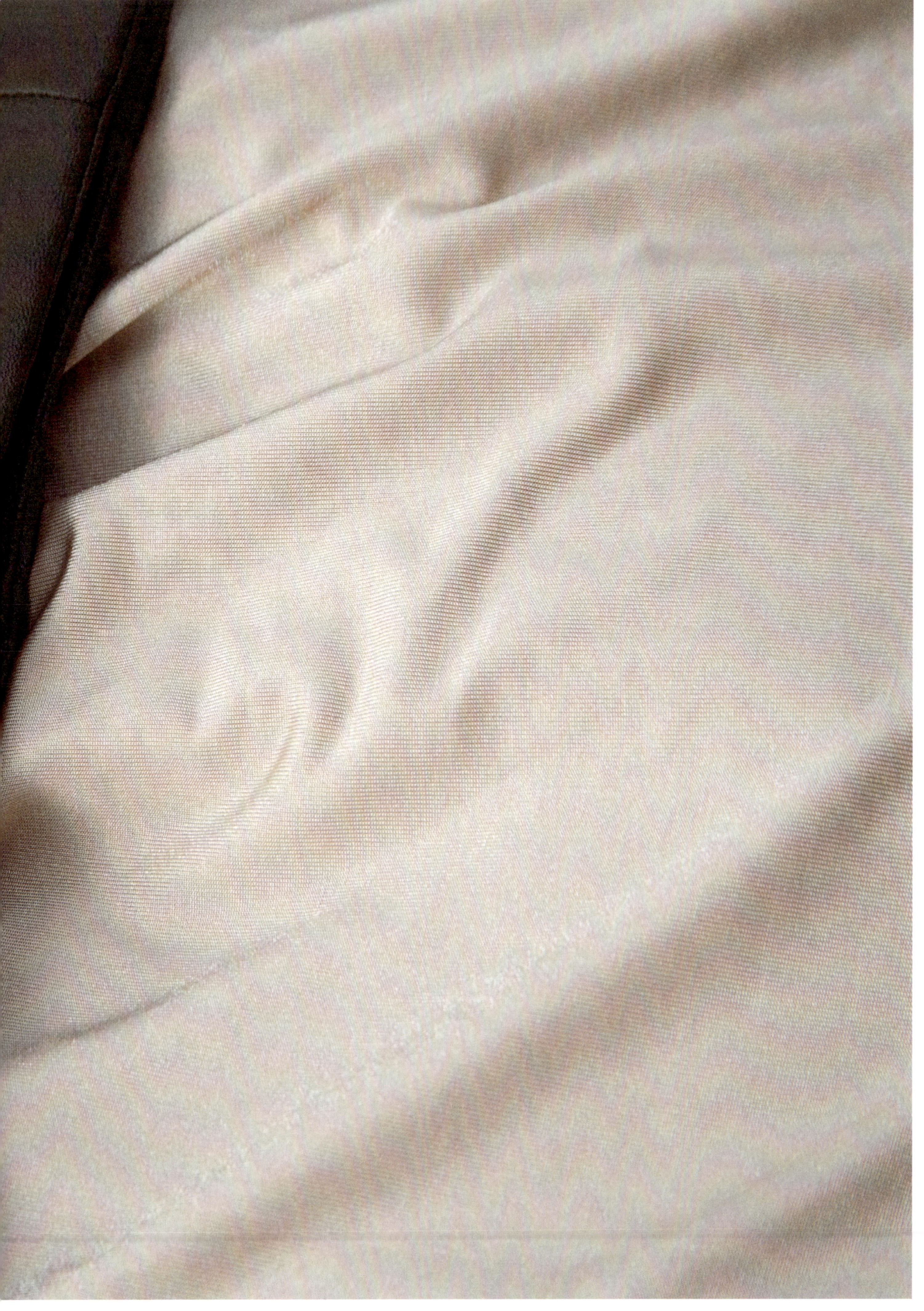

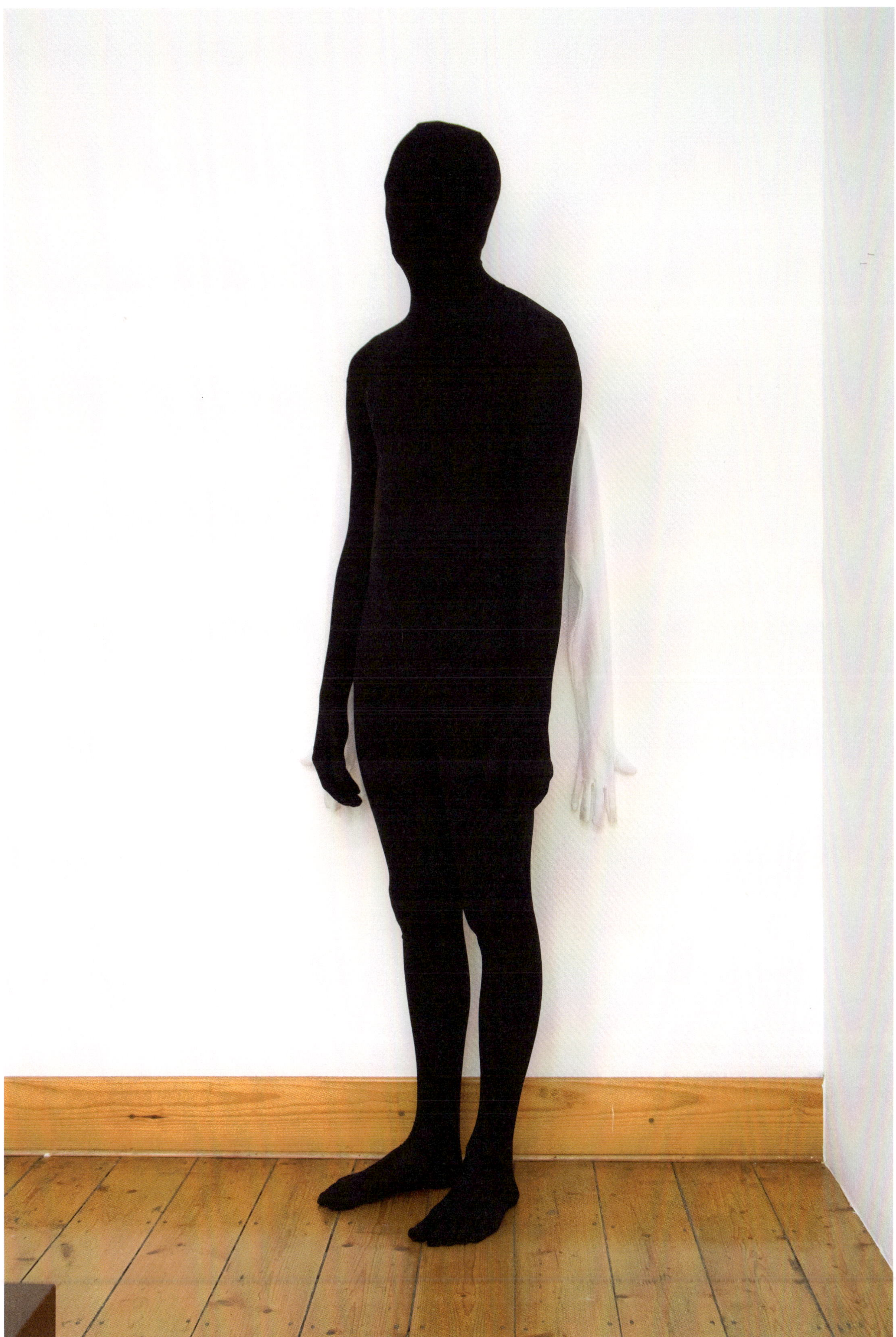

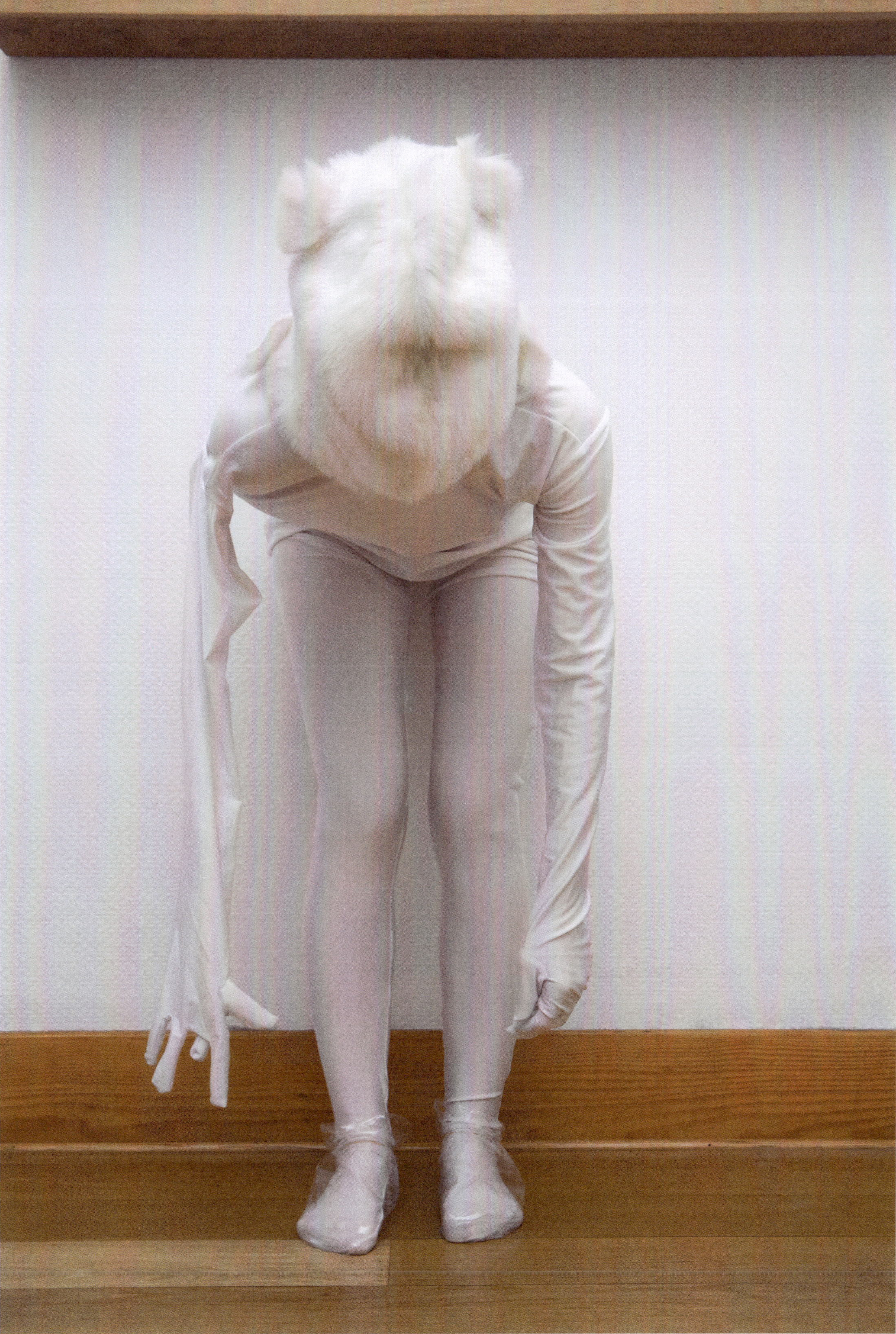

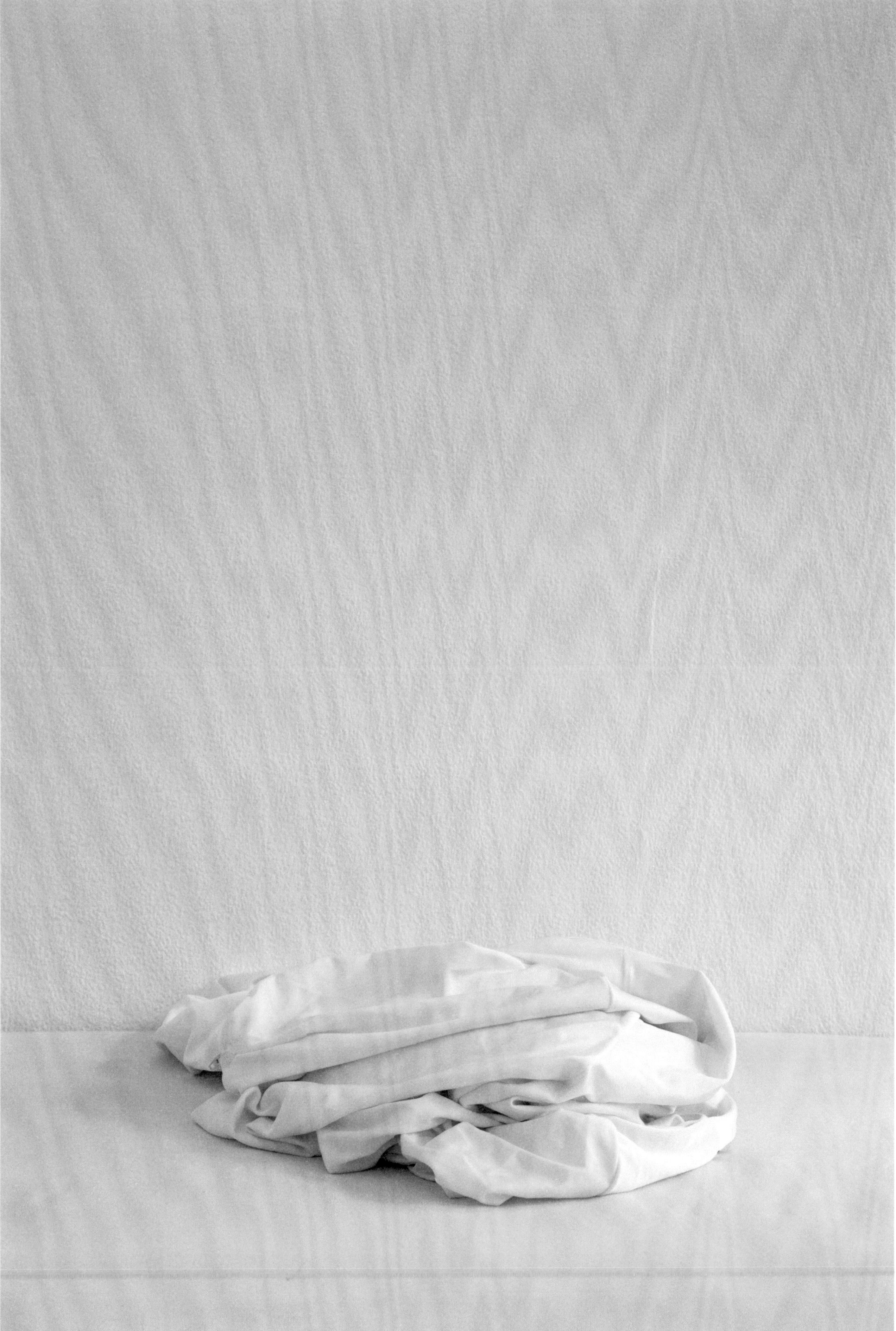

27

28 29

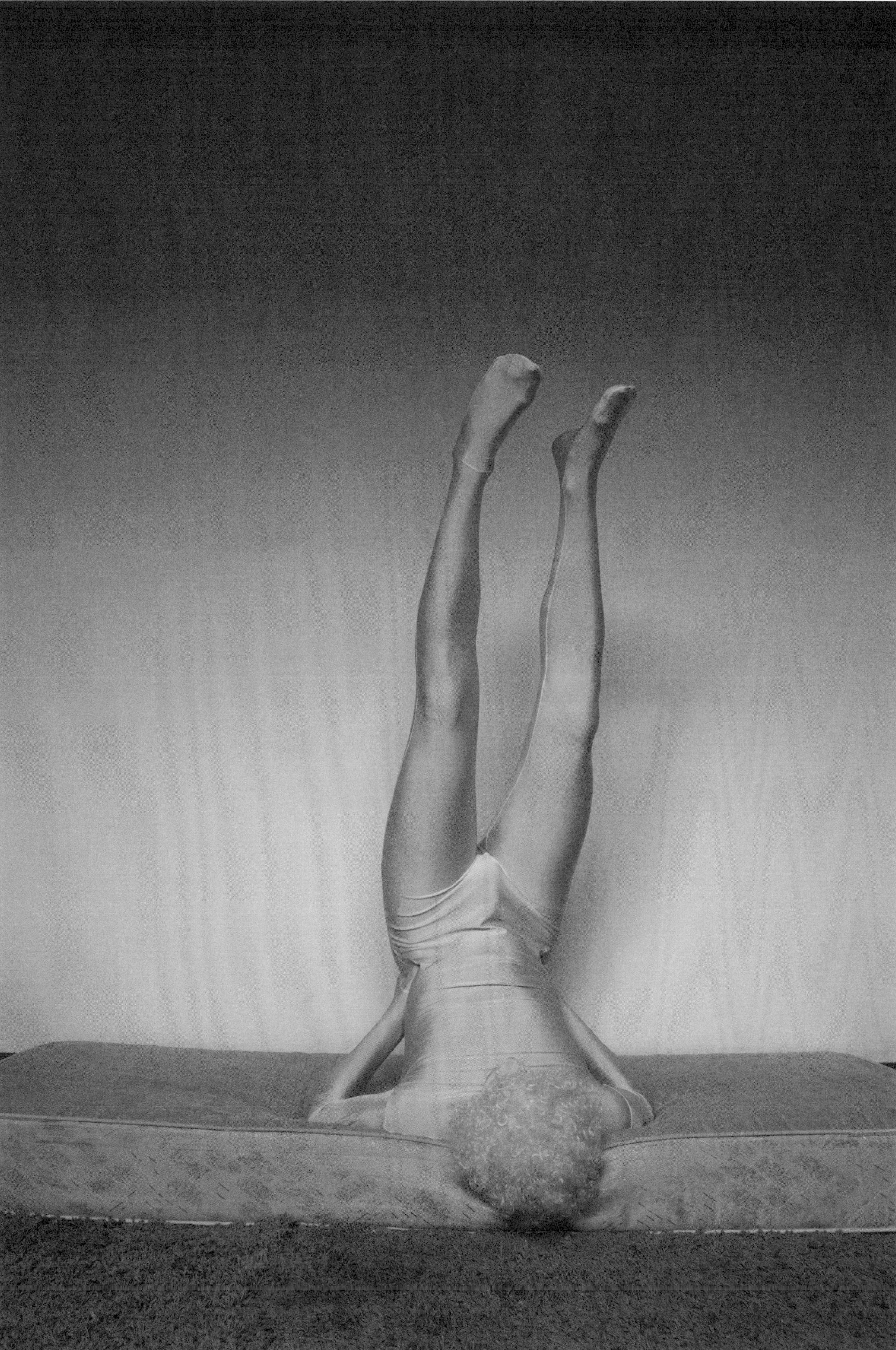

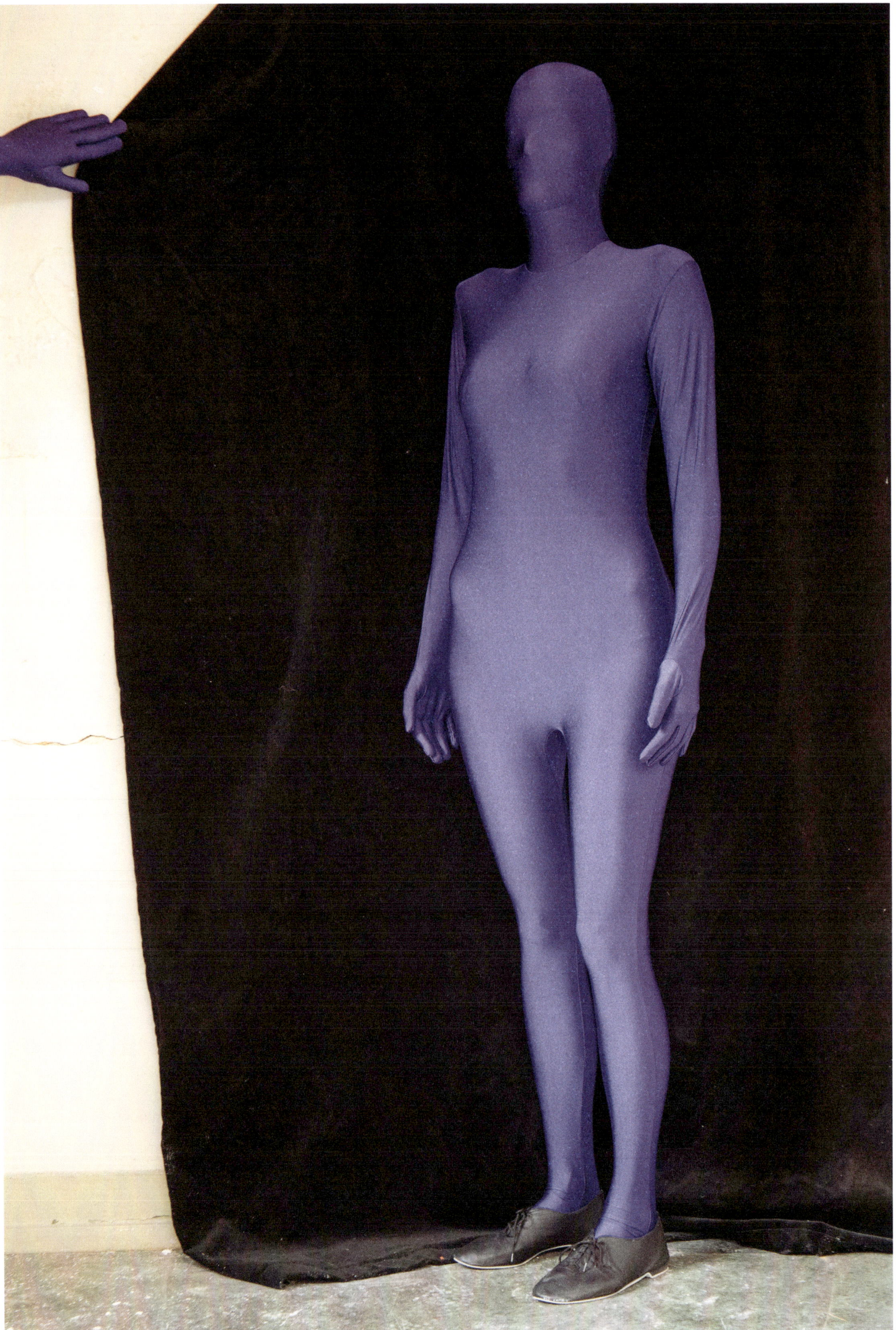

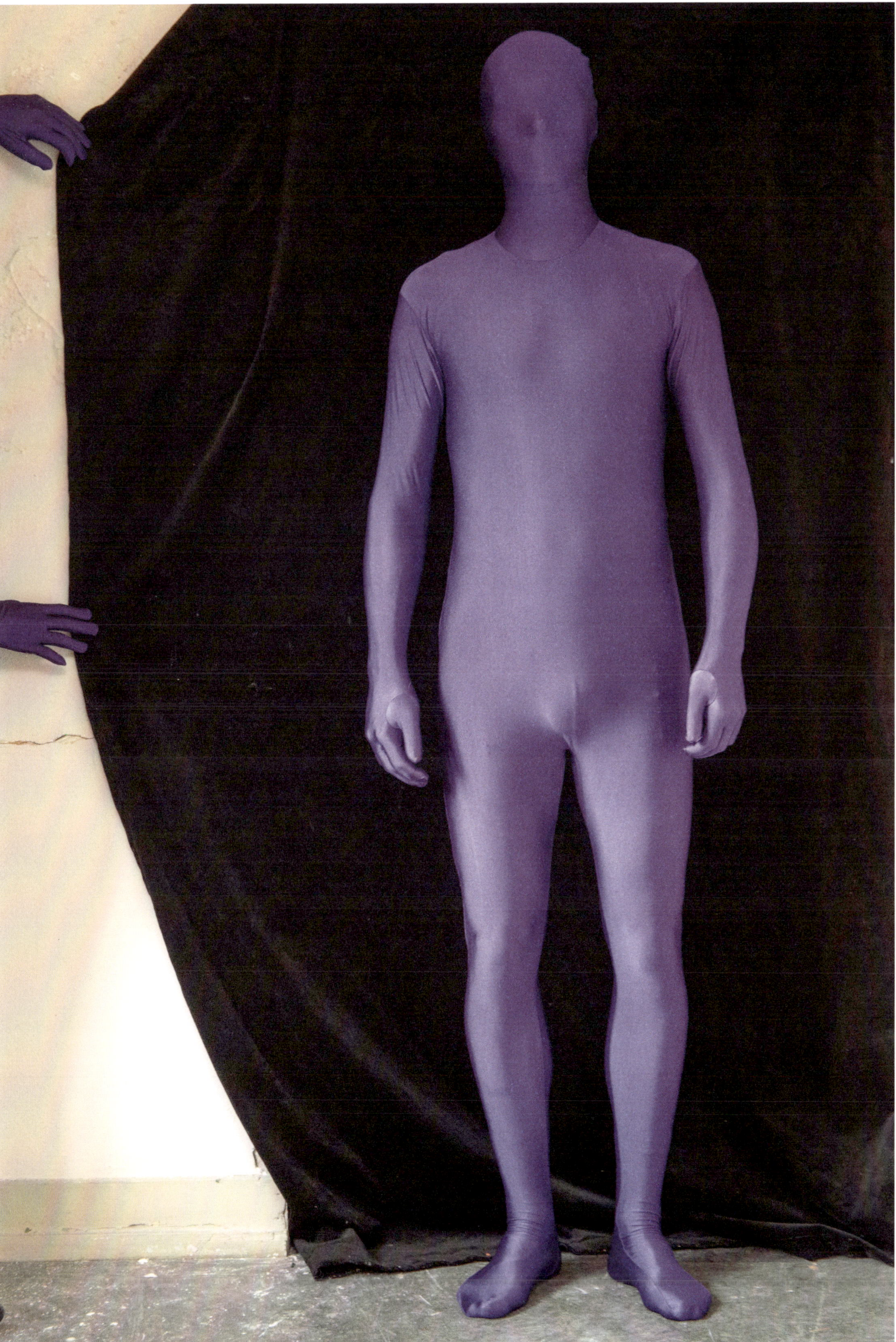

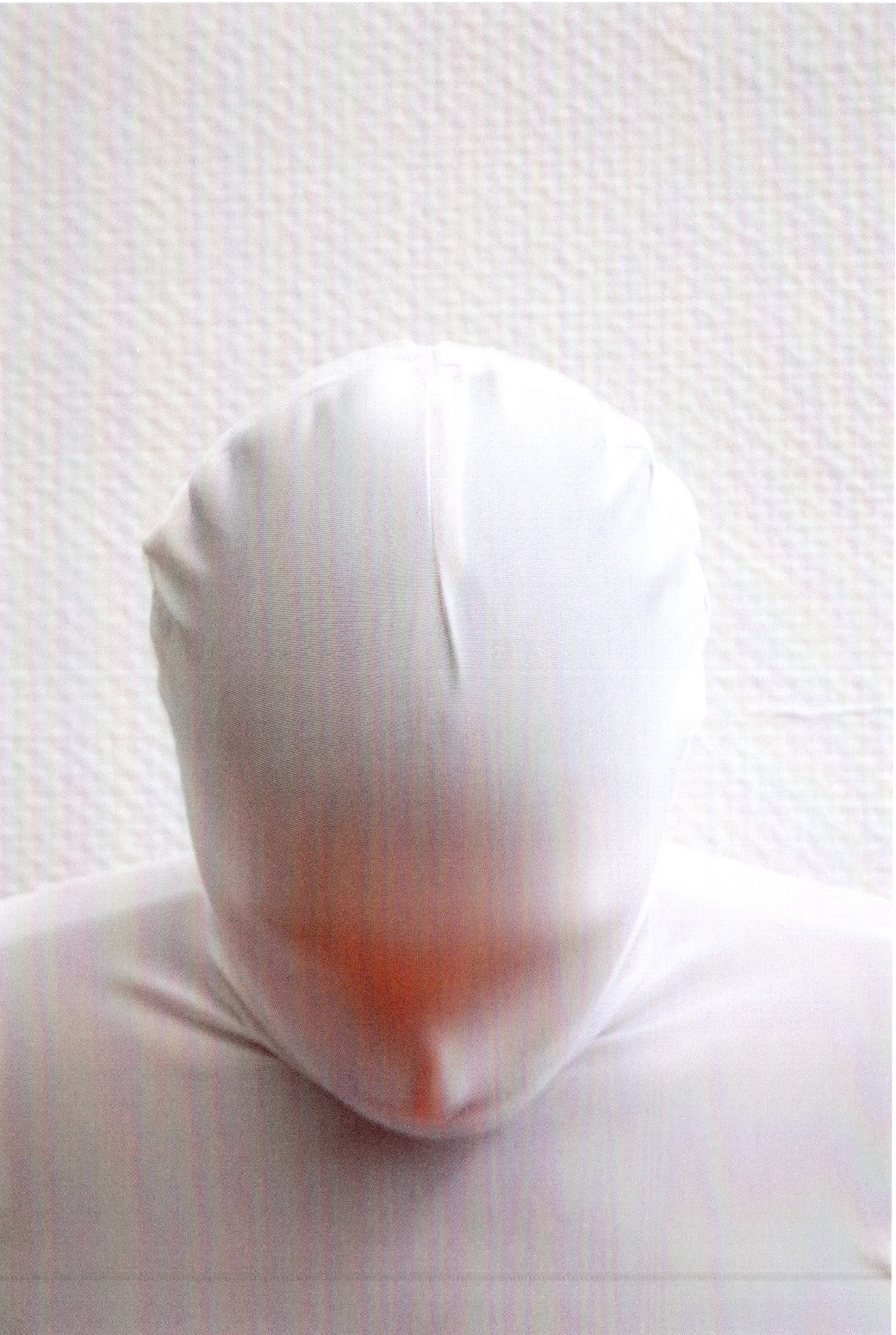

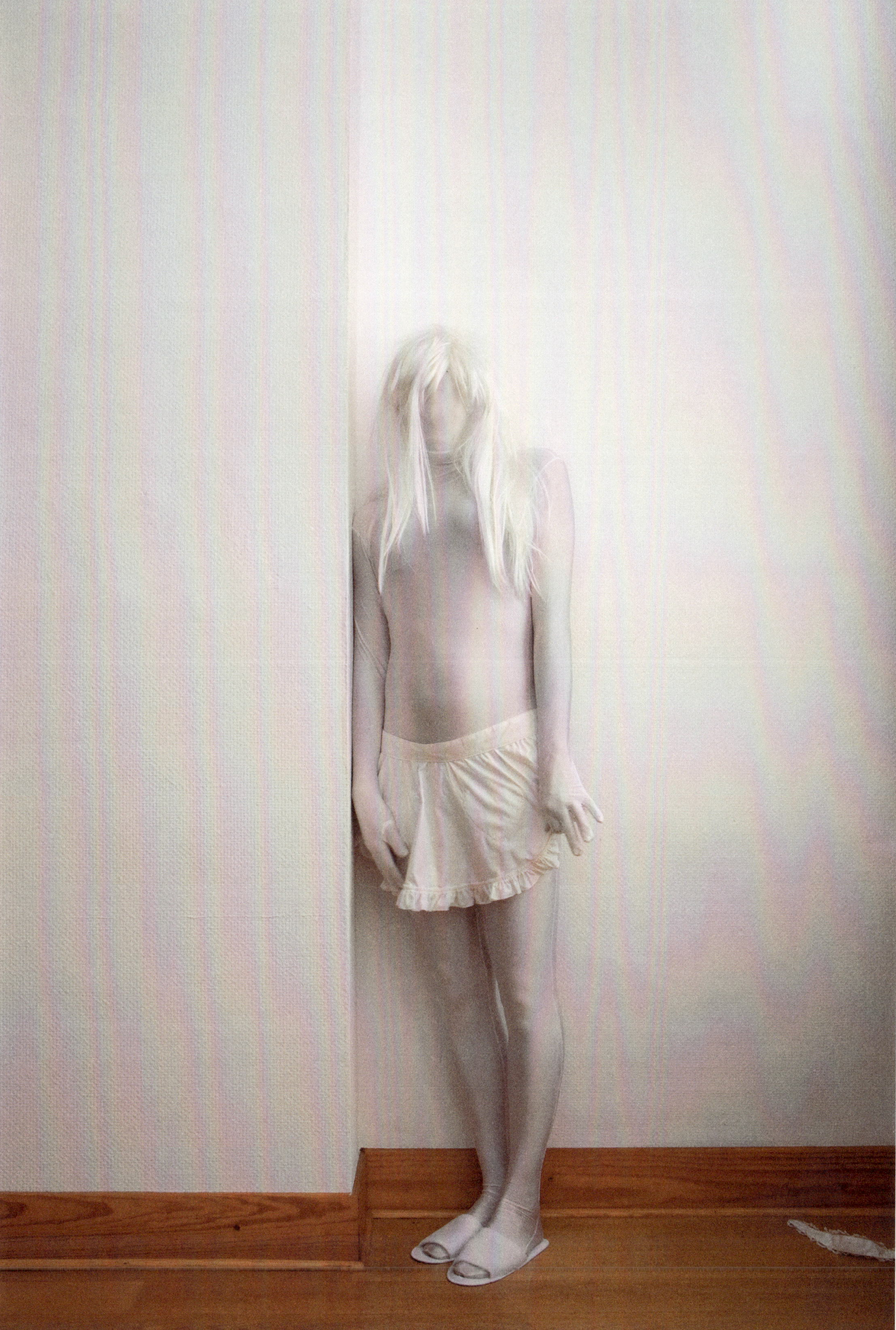

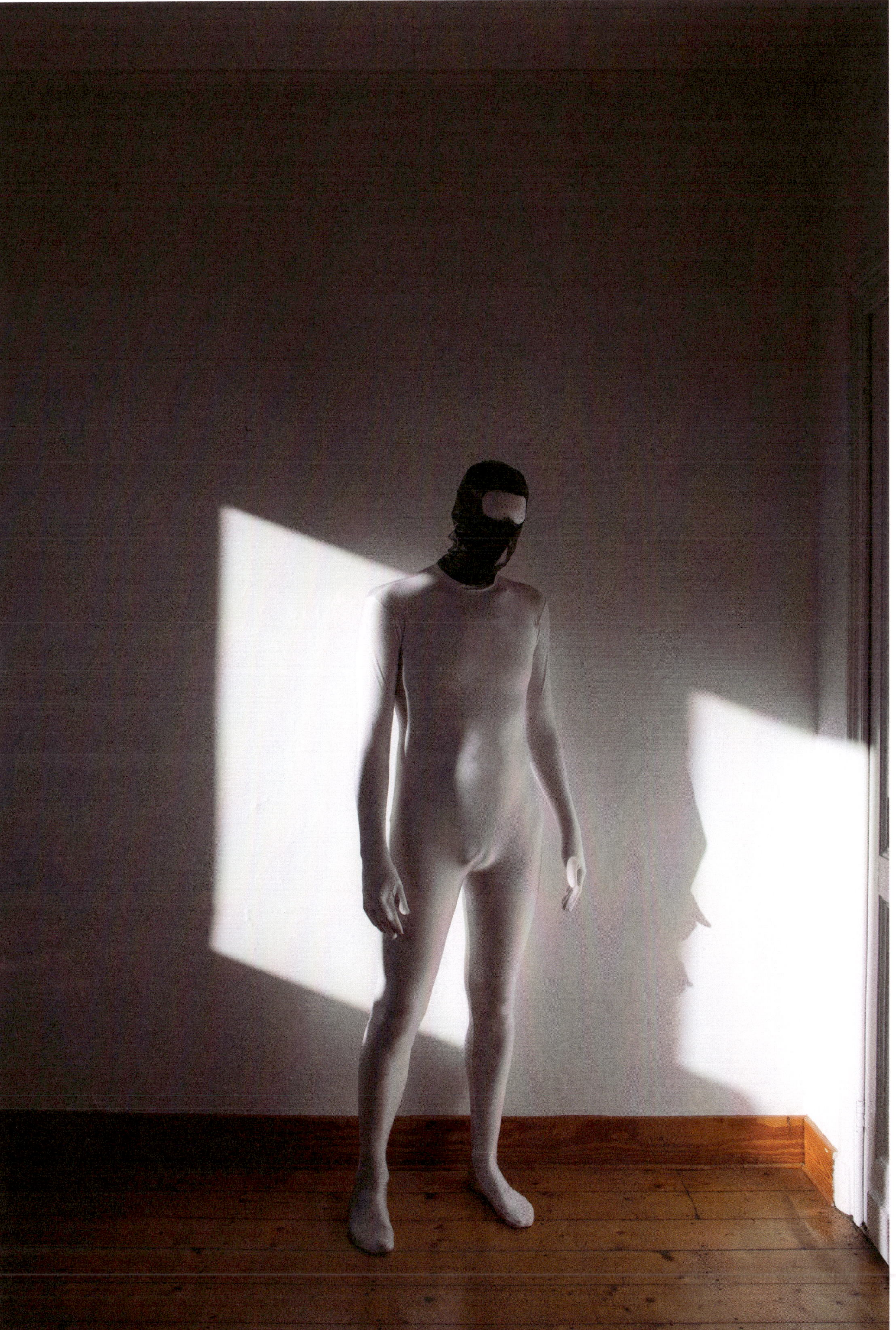

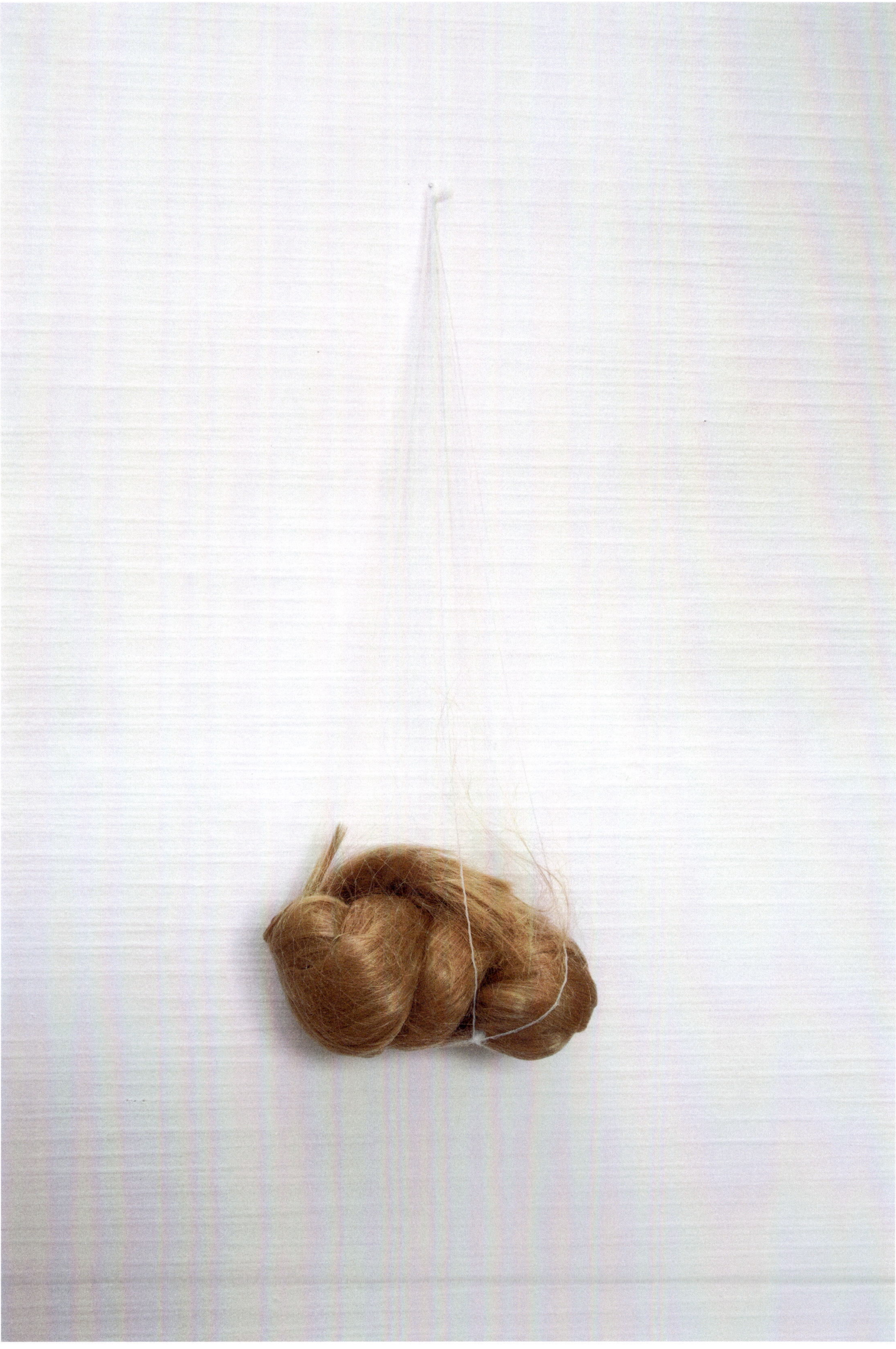

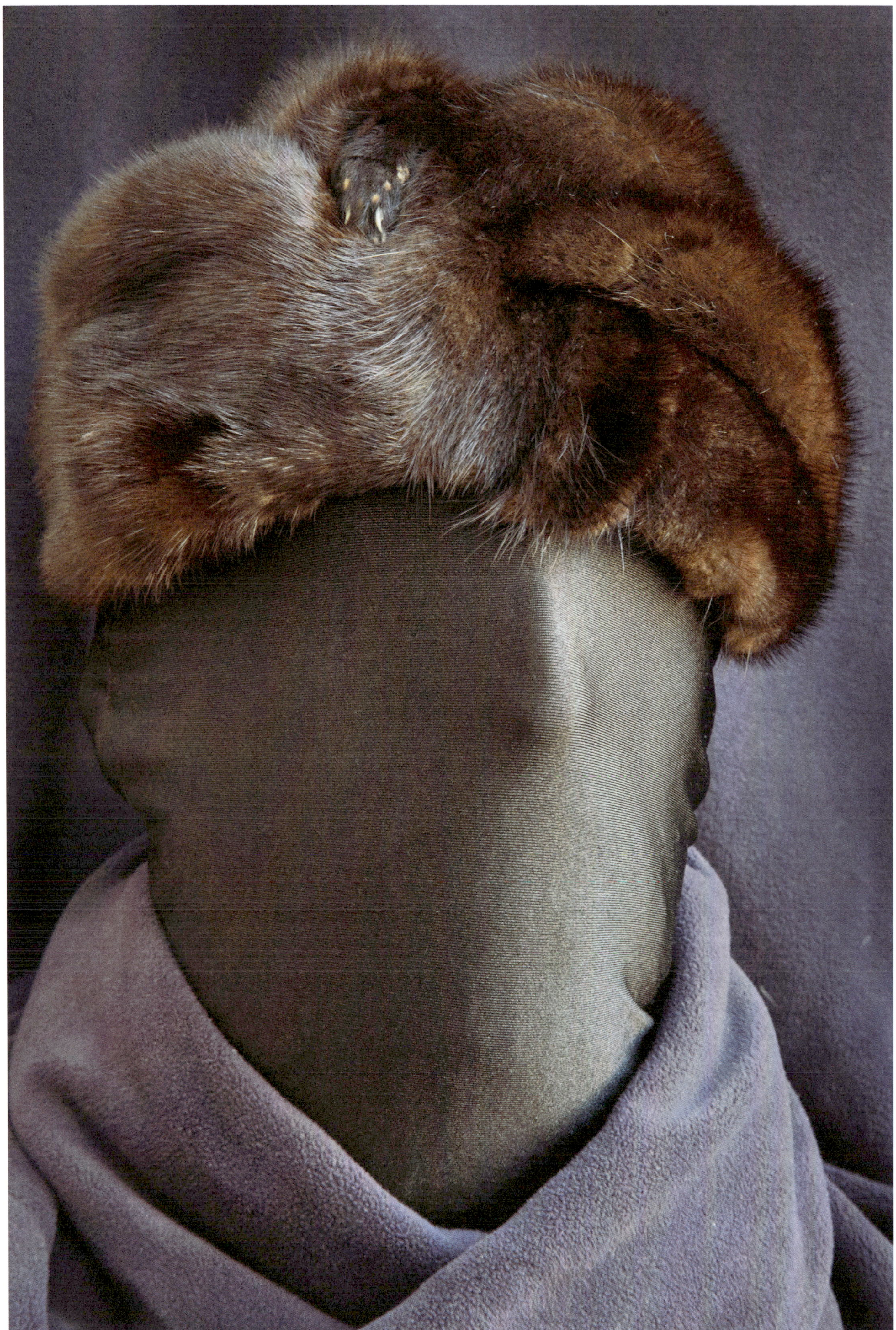

34

35 36

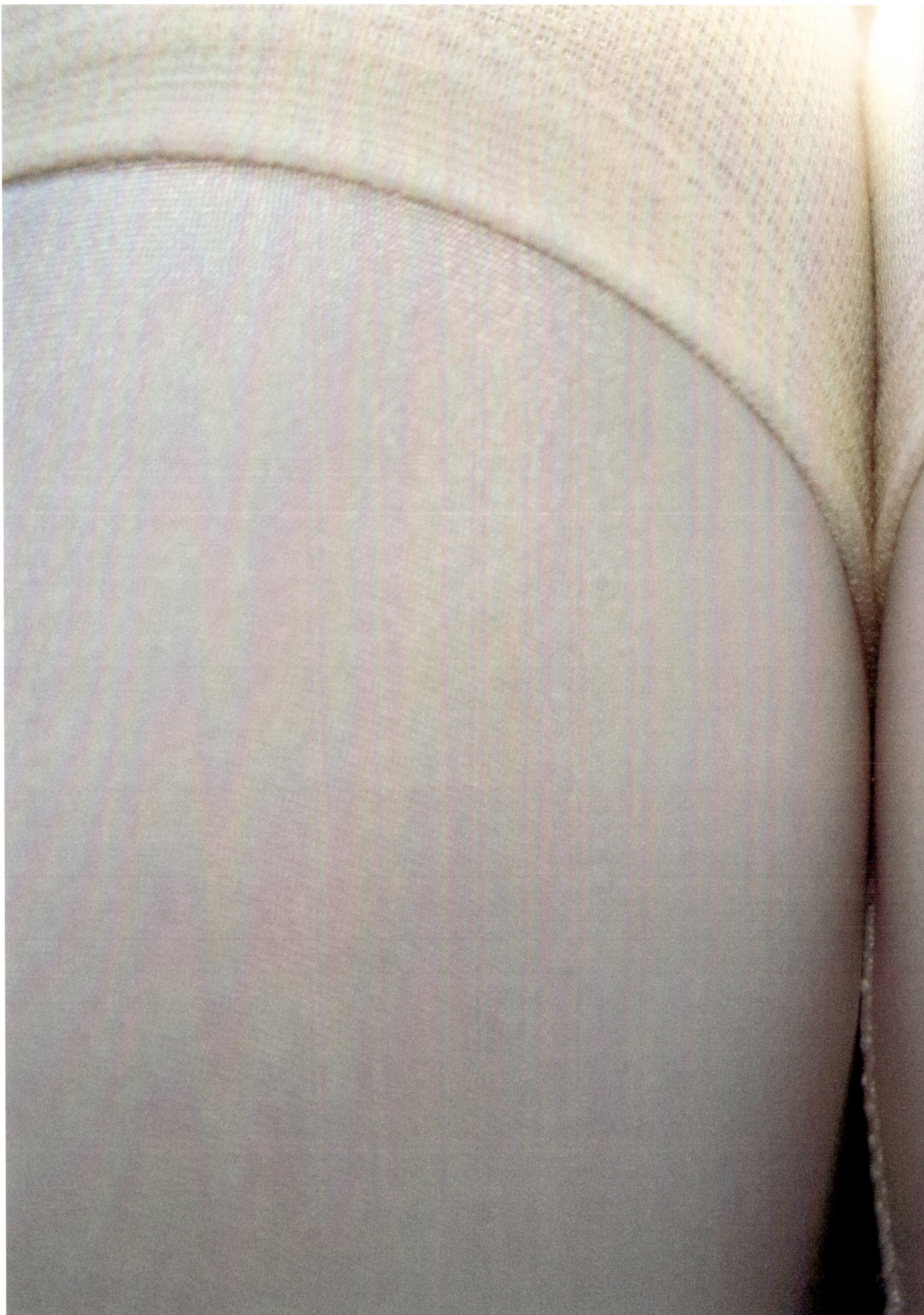

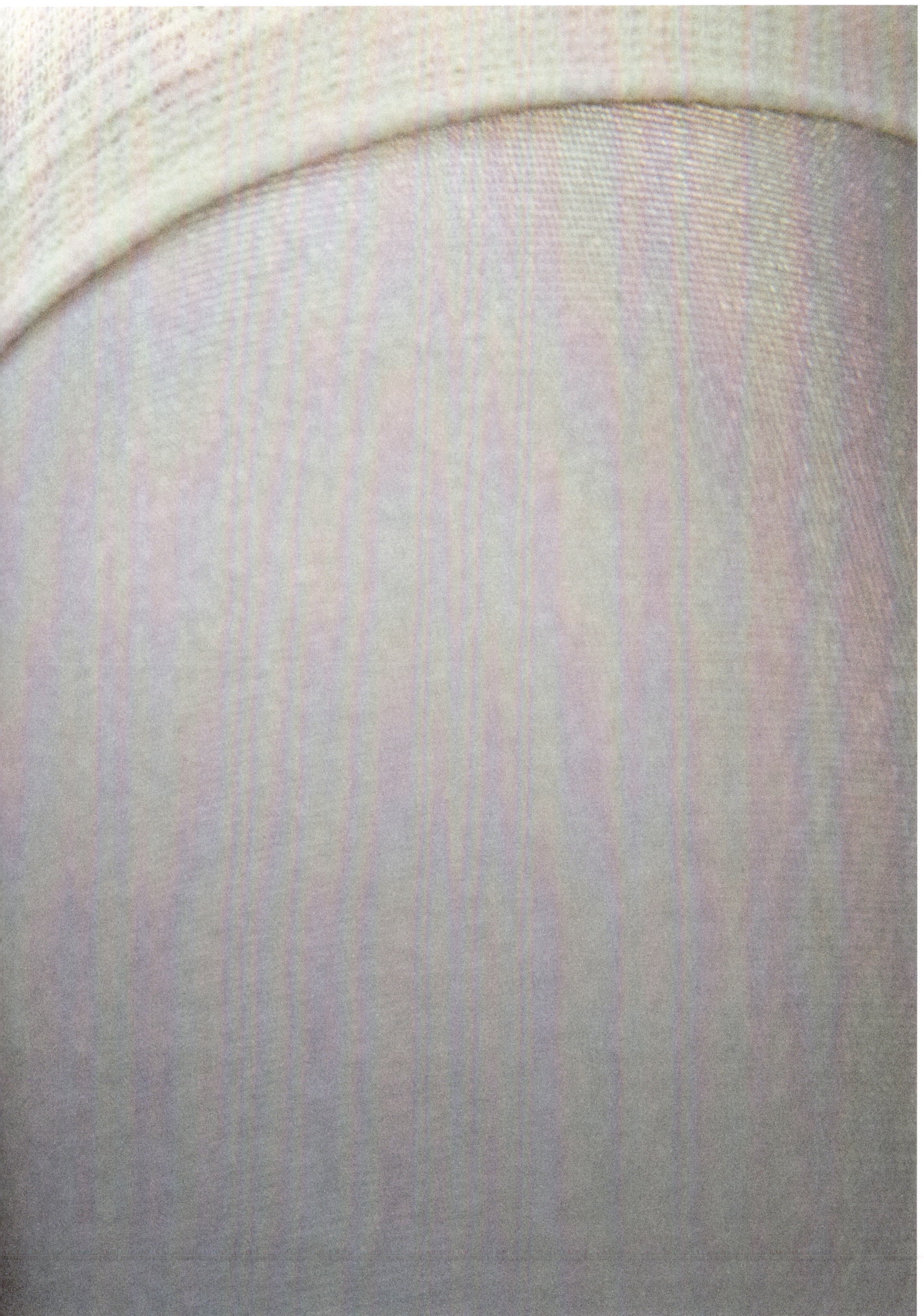

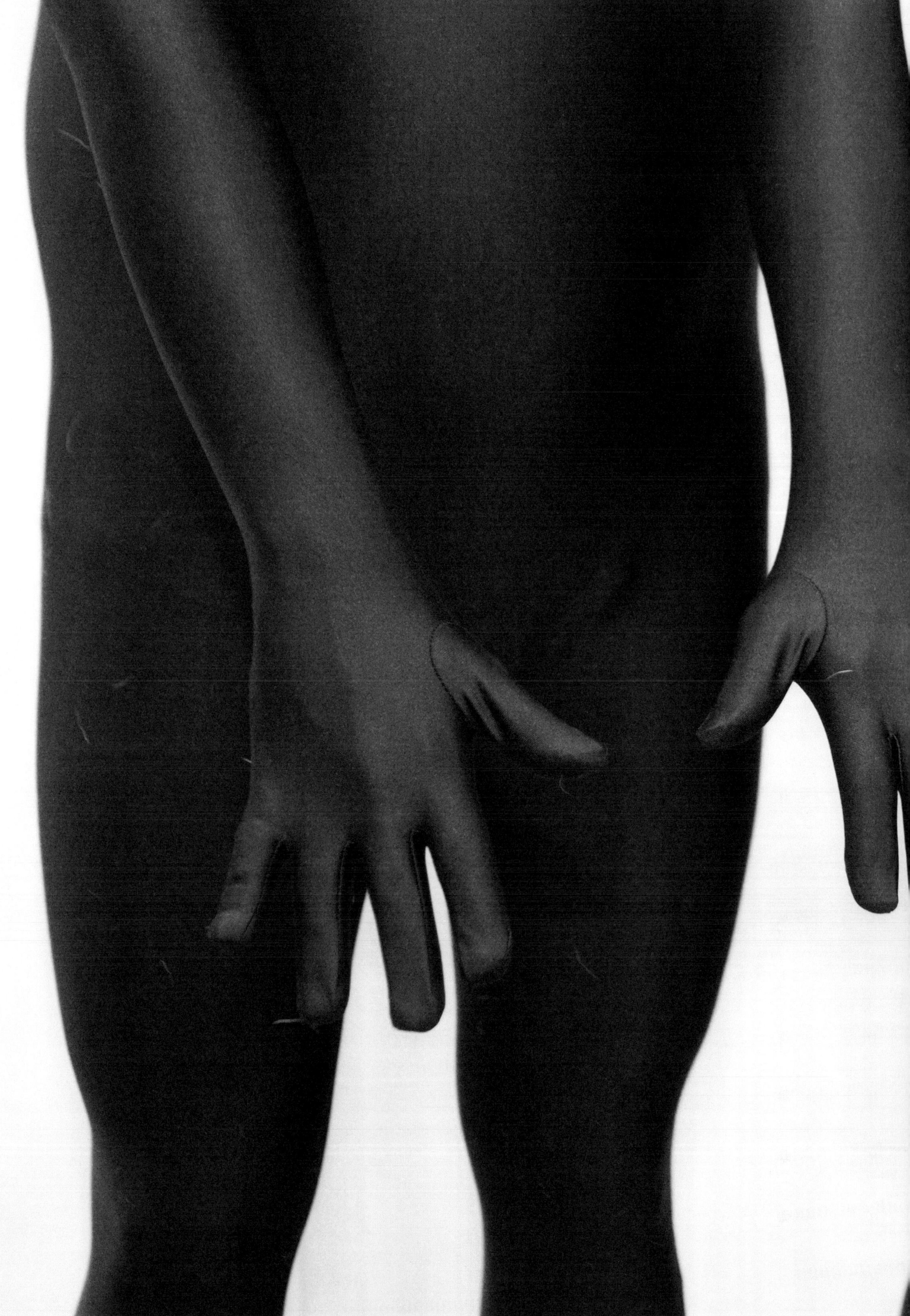

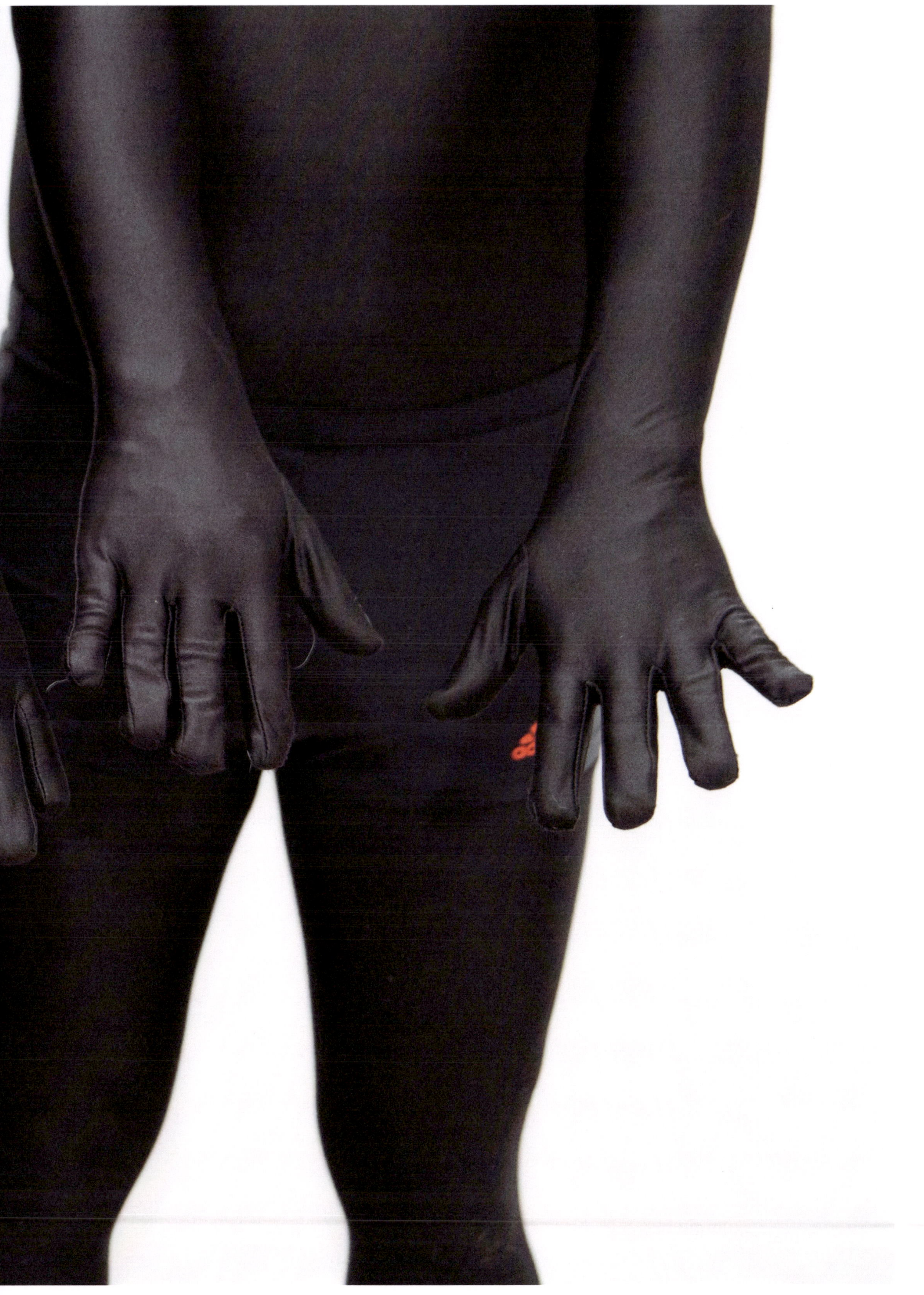

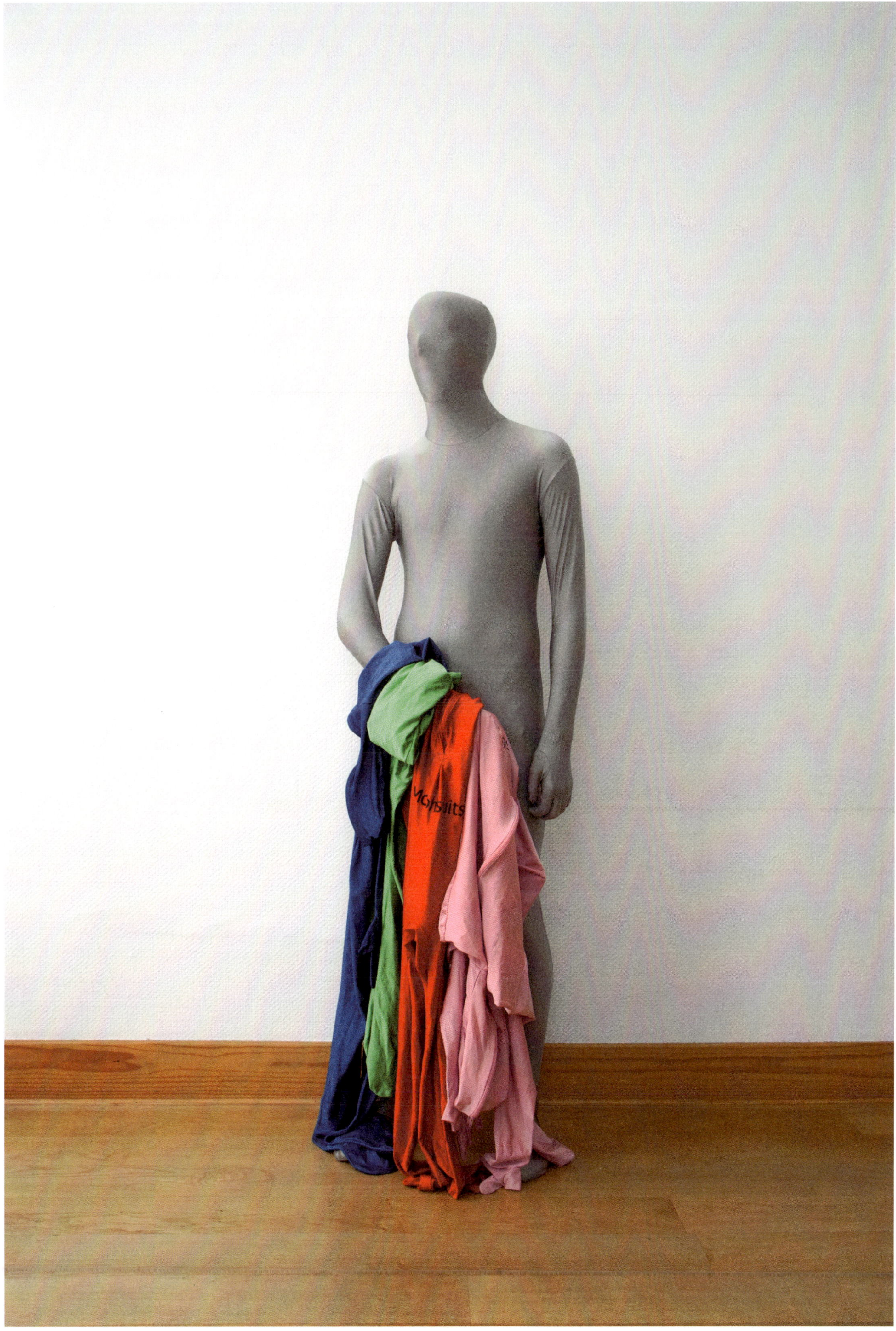

38

39 40

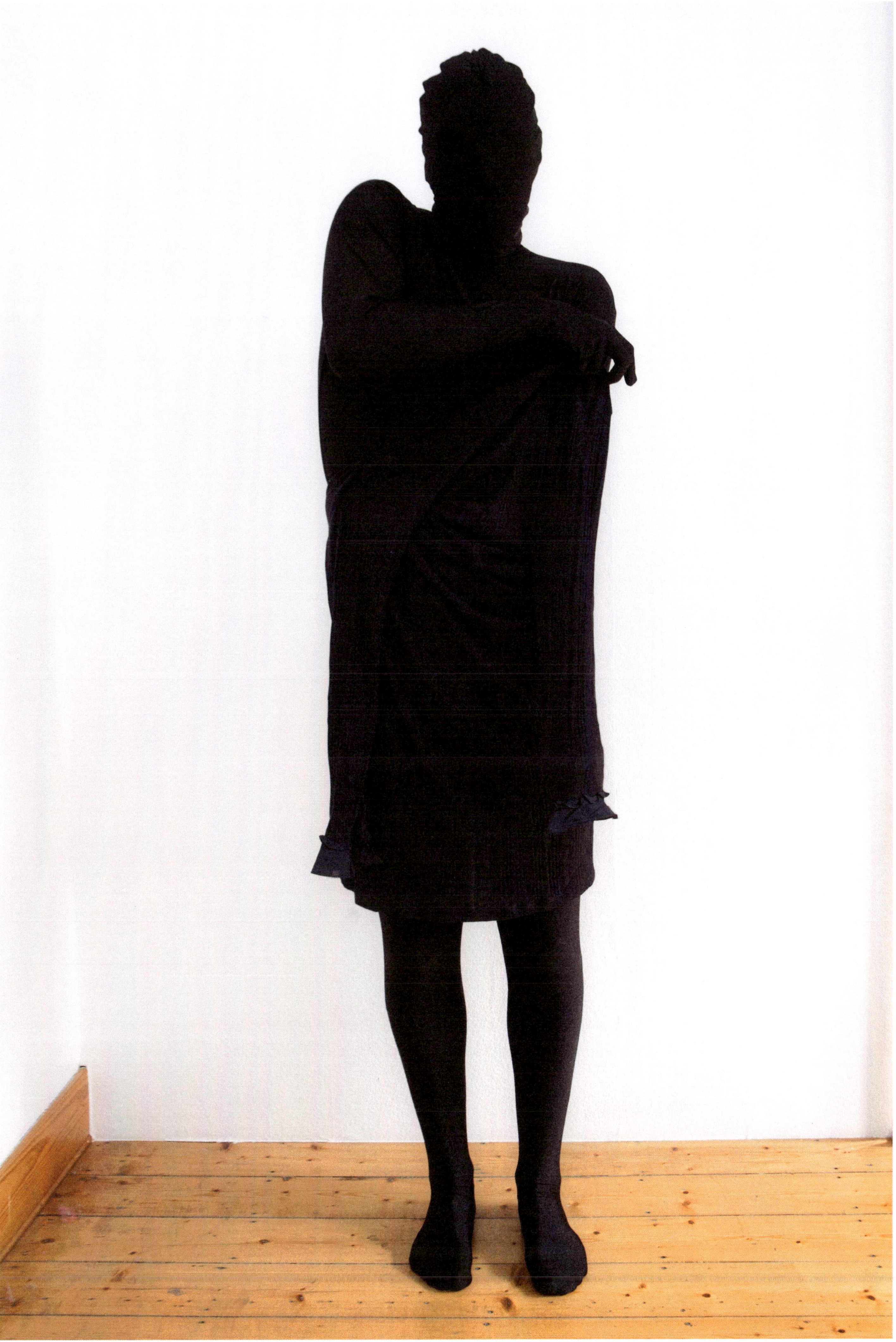

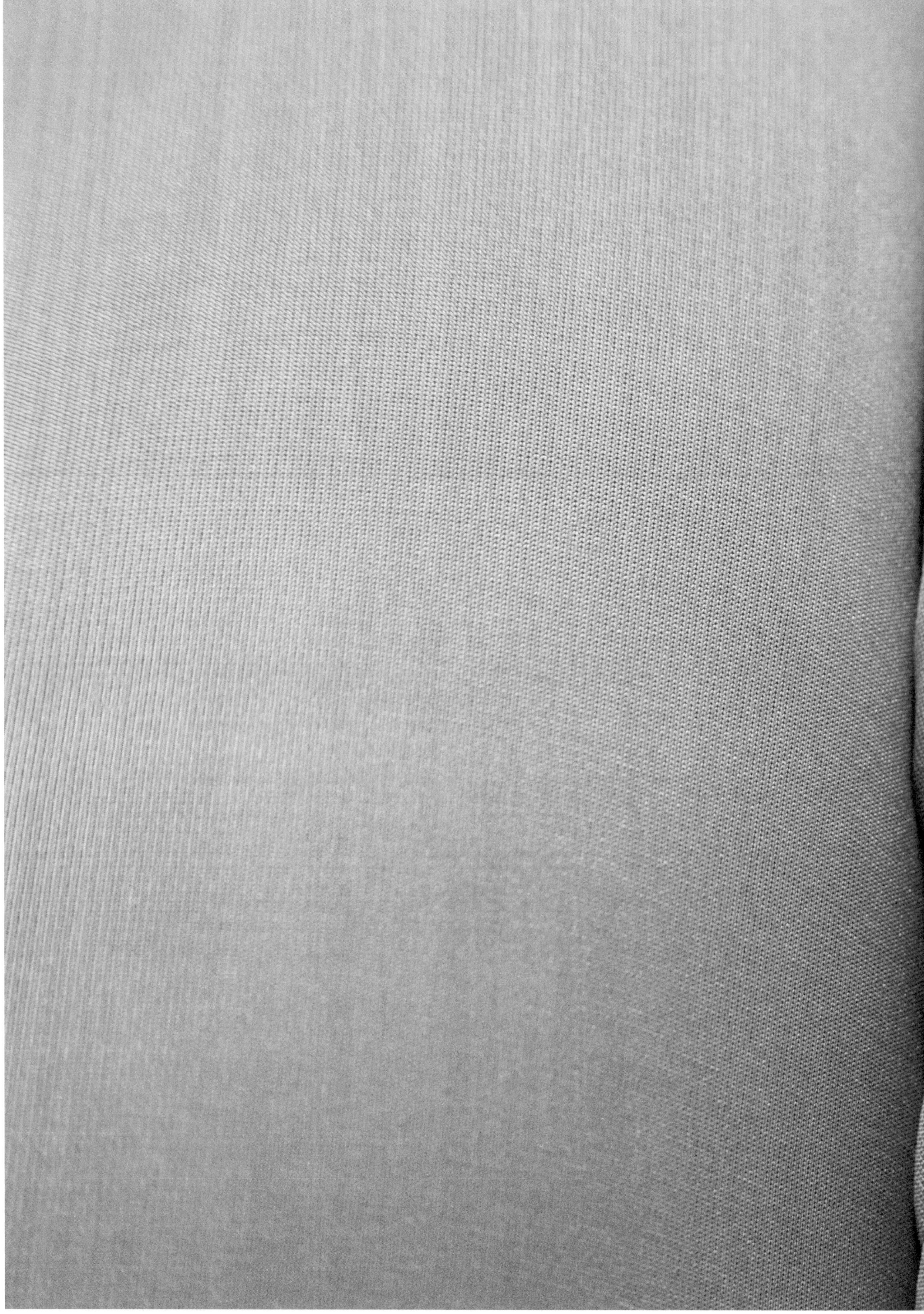

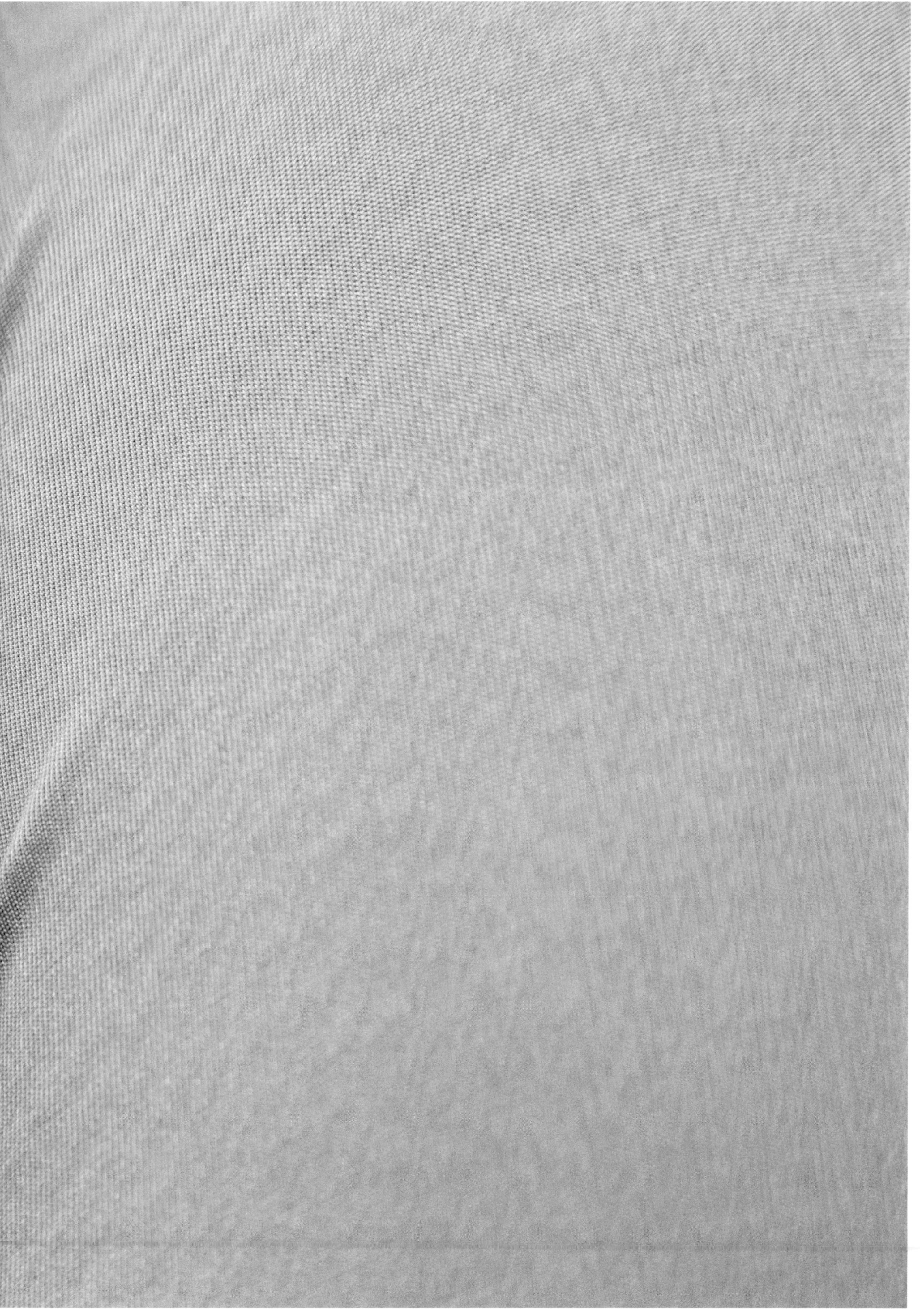

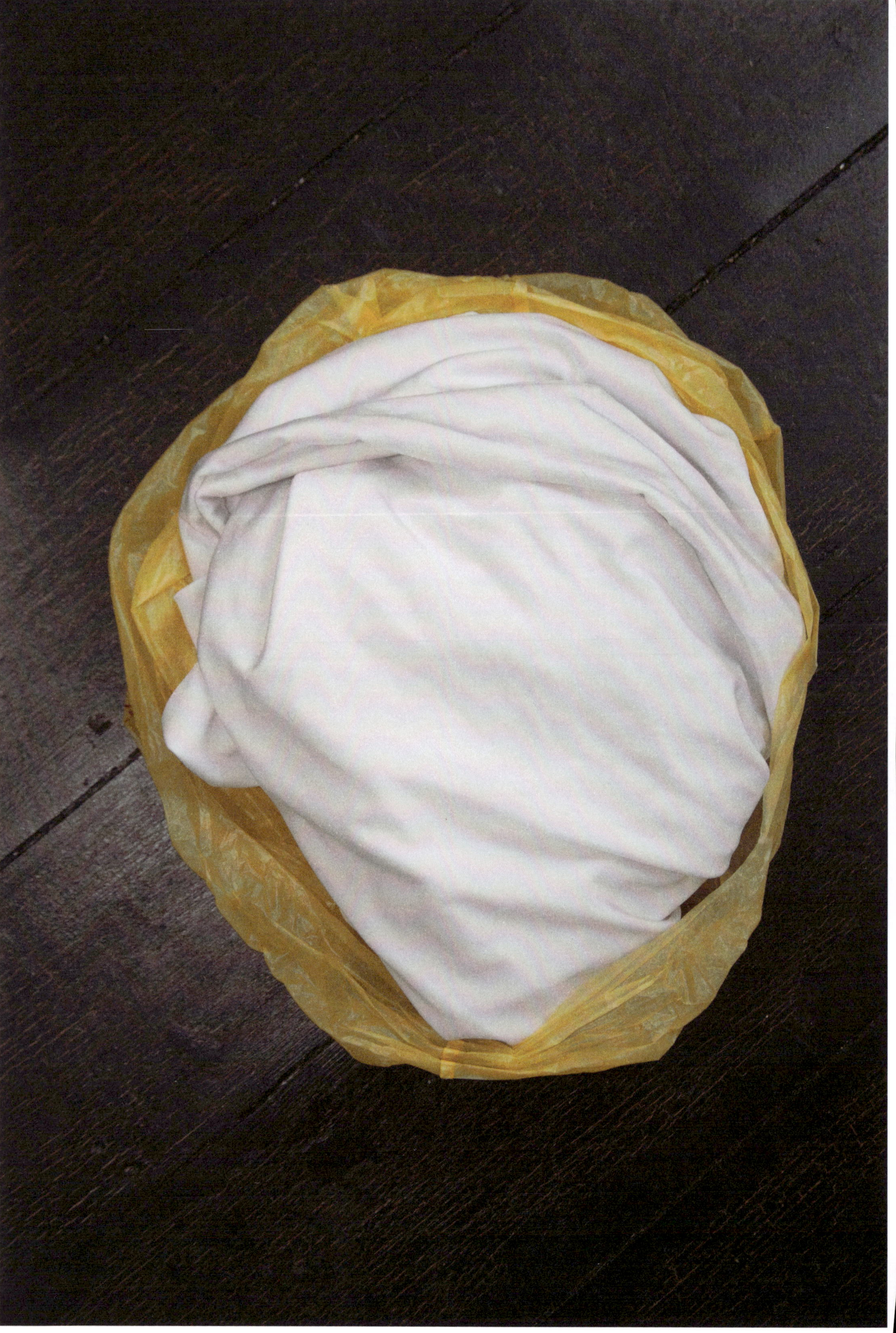